The Richardson Years: 1966-1982

The Richardson Years: 1966-1982

by Carol S. Dodd

Published by the University of Hawaii Foundation

Designed by Clarence Lee
Manufactured in the United States of America

Library of Congress No. 84–51656

Distributed by University of Hawaii Press:
Order Department
University of Hawaii Press
2840 Kolowalu Street
Honolulu, Hawaii 96822

ISBN 0–8248–0988–2

Contents

Foreword

My wife and I first met Bill and Amy Richardson in the 1950s and were immediately attracted by their down-to-earth friendliness and their attitudes toward each other and their children. It is from this viewpoint that I continue to see Bill Richardson and from which I write this foreword. He is, to me, not the ex-Chief Justice of Hawaii, not the ex-Lieutenant Governor, not a Trustee of Bishop Estate. He is a friend.

James Michener's sometimes provocative book, *Hawaii,* contains a few paragraphs about "the golden men," a concept a "group of sociologists in Hawaii were perfecting . . . that . . . suggested a new type of man was being developed. He was a man influenced by both the west and the east, a man at home in either the business councils of New York, or the philosophical retreats of Kyoto, a man wholly modern and American, yet in tune with the ancient and the Oriental. The name they invented for him was the Golden Man."

Michener observed that this "hopeful man of the future, this unique contribution to the rest of the world, did not depend for his genesis upon racial intermarriage at all. He was a product of the mind."

From my friend's eyeview, Bill Richardson is one of "the golden men" of the Hawaiian Islands. He sees what is happening from a position containing ingredients from a variety of cultures, of attitudes, and senses of pace and time. He takes advantage of our remote location to avoid the rush of events and to approach his life from a distance from the conventional current wisdom.

This book's emphasis is on the time from 1966–1982, years during which Bill Richardson led Hawaii's Supreme Court. I leave for others to evaluate his work as a judge and a Chief Justice, but I note that the National Center for State Courts recently dedicated the "Richardson Board Rooms" at their national headquarters in Williamsburg, Virginia.

I have learned much about Hawaii and about William Shaw Richardson from Carol Santoki Dodd's straightforward, cogent story. She brings a sound training in literature and education to her task. I commend her readable book to you.

Herbert C. Cornuelle

Honolulu
July 2, 1984

"The man who is Chief Justice must balance the rules of the past to conform with the state of society today. He must bring the old rules in line with modern times. He must remember that those rules were made under a different structure."

"He must live in the past—but not only the past. He must adopt the fundamental principles of the past and bring them into focus with the present."

William Shaw Richardson, Chief Justice, State of Hawaii, 1966–1982
February 26, 1966[1]

I
The Commission as Chief Justice

The dawn over the island chain was still and clear.

On that morning of March 25, 1966, newspaper reporters —an objective and questioning lot at best—wrote remarkably effusive lines about the flower-scented air and the brilliance of the skies over Iolani Palace. The Palace had served as monarchial home of Hawaii's rulers from 1821 to 1893, then as capitol for the Republic, the Territory, and the State until the time that a new state capitol was completed in 1969.

The reporters were even more enthusiastic in their descriptions of the ceremony which took place in the Throne Room of the Palace that morning.

Precisely at ten-thirty, William Shaw Richardson was escorted from his second-floor Office of the Lieutenant Governor, past the bottom of the stairway where two Royal Guards stood at attention, and into the Throne Room crowded with family, State officials, members of the Bar, and many other well-wishers.

The ceremony which commissioned Richardson as Chief Justice of the State of Hawaii had special meaning for those who knew the ancient Hawaiian past as well as the more recent political history of the islands. They found the juxtaposition of past and present strangely moving.

Empty thrones under a red canopy dominated the front of the room; they were flanked by *kahilis*, feather standards which were symbols of royalty. The thrones had been occupied by King Kalakaua and his consort Kapiolani, later by Queen Liliuokalani until the last sad days of her reign just before the turn of the century. Draped with a lei of fragrant *maile* leaves, a portrait of Jonah Kalanianaole Kuhio seemed to epitomize Hawaiian royalty. Prince Kuhio, complex Delegate to Congress from 1903 to 1922, had been at once convivial, imperious, ambivalent in his feelings toward *haoles* while trying to work with them in the interests of his people.[2]

Overhead in the chambers, faceted chandeliers bespoke a more elegant, leisurely era of rulers. Outside on the lanai, Hawaiian and part-Hawaiian students from Kamehameha Schools raised their voices in song. And throughout the Throne Room, the multi-racial faces among participants and observers alike were eloquent proof of a new Hawaii.

Not only was there visual juxtaposition of past and present, the music that day resounded with echoes of the past while it also told of recent island commitment to America as its youngest member state: the Queen's Prayer, that poignant and beautiful song written by Liliuokalani; the Star-Spangled Banner; Hawaii Ponoi, written by Kalakaua as Hawaii's national anthem and now its state song.

Only a few observers that morning knew that as Lieutenant Governor, Bill Richardson occupied the same room that had served as Queen Liliuokalani's quarters while she awaited trial for misprison of treason against the Republic of Hawaii. Fewer still knew that in an earlier time, mischievous children had been punished by confinement to an alcove above Richardson's office; his own grandmother, irrepressible Kaula Shaw, had been sent to this very alcove when she misbehaved. For those who knew, the reasonance between past and present gave added dimension to the morning's program.

During the brief ceremony, Governor John Anthony Burns spoke of the qualities of his appointee: "By all critieria—by temperament, by his professional and educational background, and by his historic family ties—Bill Richardson is admirably equipped to assume leadership of our judicial system."[3]

Then he added a statement which may have seemed quite ordinary to some, but which held deep meaning for others in the audience: "It is my hope that this appointment will further inspire the youth of Hawaii and all our citizens, for there is no limit to the heights each of us can reach if we but apply our rich native talents and abilities."[4]

In the audience that morning were many members of the small vanguard which had begun the modern Democratic Party in Hawaii over two decades before. Burns himself was acknowledged as their leader. Richardson, a close Burns ally, had been Party secretary, then chairman of the Central Committee for three terms before winning election as Burns' Lieutenant Governor in 1962.

The vanguard's battle had been against an entrenched autocracy which found it difficult to accept immigrant Asiatics and even native Hawaiians on equal terms. The Governor's allusion to unbounded heights might seem typical of such installation ceremonies, but to members of the early corps of Democrats, those words signalled a battle won.

Photos taken after the ceremony show Governor Burns and Bill Richardson walking down the steps of the Palace, through a corridor of Royal Guards spaced between Iolani Palace and Ali'iolani Hale, Hawaii's historic judiciary building. The Governor's usual stoic mien is replaced by smiles. Richardson strides confidently. They seem attuned to one another, these two comrades for many years.

Directly behind them is Bill Richardson's wife, Amy, her simple outfit complete with gloves and a hat of spring flowers. On one side of her is William L. Fleming, president of the State Bar; on the other side is Bert T. Kobayashi, Sr., a Harvard-educated lawyer and the State's Attorney General, who—by that group's own consensus—was among the most able of Burns' first cabinet. Behind them are the Richardson children: William Kahelelani, then 10; Barbara Piimaile, 13; and Corinne Kahaulani, 15. Also in the entourage are Democratic office-holders: Tadao Beppu, George Ariyoshi, John Ushijima. Like the morning, their faces are clear, untroubled, and young with promise.

Led by the Governor and his newly commissioned Chief Justice, the entourage walks across King Street, past the statue of King Kamehameha I, and into a crowded courtroom on the second floor of Ali'iolani Hale. During the ceremony conducted at Iolani Palace, Richardson had received the Governor's commission to become Chief Justice; now he would take an oath of office administered by Acting Chief Justice Charles E. Cassidy. Gus Sproat, attendant to every Chief Justice for the last forty years, robes Chief Justice Richardson, then leads him to the middle seat of the five-member court. Those who flank him are Associate Justices Cassidy, Rhoda V. Lewis, Jack H. Mizuha and Cable A. Wirtz.

The editorial pages of both Honolulu newspapers carry words of praise the next day. The *Advertiser* writes: "He [Richardson] is an official who takes his responsibilities with full seriousness. We are confident that on the bench he will sustain his pledge to work 'in the finest traditions of human jurisprudence.' "[5] The *Honolulu Star-Bulletin* states: "[The appointment] puts at the head of the courts a widely respected moderate of unchallenged integrity who seems to be satisfactory to Democrats and Republicans alike."[6]

As perfect as the first day of the seven-year term was, John Burns' nomination of Bill Richardson was not unmarred by controversy.

As early as May of 1965, Burns had talked informally with certain members of the press. The Governor habitually kept his own counsel except, of course, when it did not suit his purposes. During this conversation, he apparently leaked the possibility of naming Richardson to a judgeship. Late in December of that year, after Chief Justice Wilfred C. Tsukiyama announced his intention to retire because of illness, Burns hinted to newsmen that he might name Richardson to fill the post.[7]

In retrospect, Richardson himself remembered that the Governor approached him on the last possible day a nomination could be presented to the Senate for its approval during the 1966 legislative session.

"What's this talk I hear about your becoming Chief Justice?" Burns asked at that point. Although the Governor suffered a public reputation as The Great Stone Face, his sense of humour was quick and well-honed, surfacing in small groups and comfortable situations.

Richardson answered in the same light yet serious tone which sometimes marked conversations between the two men.

"You know as much about it as I do, Mr. Governor."

The Governor then queried, "What does Amy think?"

Richardson replied, "Why don't you call and ask her?"

Amy was ecstatic.

It was no secret that she disliked the fawning that typically accompanied political campaigns. She and her mother-in-law, also named Amy, often sympathized with each other about the miseries of political life: they saw that politics could disrupt family life; that any tough political decision brought abuse from one group of citizens or another; that the lives of politicians and their families were subject to constant, sometimes painfully close scrutiny.

Bill Richardson's wife—born Amy Corinne Ching—was direct, practical, and sure of her values. She was an admitted "homebody" whose time was devoted mainly to the care of her youngsters, the running of her home, and her interest in art and in craft work. She had taught history and English at Hana and at Farrington High School before her marriage, a combination of subjects which later served her well as she became close political advisor to her husband. In the years after her marriage, she did volunteer work with various community agencies. In family and community groups alike, her opinion counted.

In talking with Burns about his appointment of her husband as Chief Justice, Amy admitted that she had always thought of her husband as a lawyer first, even through his years in politics. She allowed that she did not relish the thought of a possible future race for the governorship, although she of course would help her husband campaign again if he wished. She added with typical understatement: "He's done all right. His decisions to seek political office must have been right for him."[8] (Indeed, except for the first time when he ran unsuccessfully for the Board of Supervisors, her husband had been front runner in every race he entered. The *Star-Bulletin* commented after one Democratic Convention that Richardson had set some kind of record for popularity, leading the ticket on every ballot where his name appeared.)[9]

When Richardson's last term as Party Chairman was over in early 1962, he had looked forward to devoting more time to his family and to his law practice. When Party members asked him to consider a candidacy for the lieutenant governor's position, neither he nor his wife had been inclined to respond very enthusiastically. However, the family tradition of public service and community involvement acted as strong inducement, offsetting Richardson's wish to be a full-time lawyer and his knowledge that he could earn a better living in private practice. Similarly, he viewed the possible Supreme Court appointment with mixed feelings: great honor, at the opportunity to serve; some misgiving, at the need to ignore his personal preference for privacy and his desire to be his own boss.

But first, before announcement of the nomination, the Governor discussed with his nominee a rumour which had surfaced. A few observers claimed that Burns was assigning Richardson to the Supreme Court to rid himself of a formidable opponent in the next gubernatorial election. The two men enjoyed a fairly candid relationship, and both felt that the rumour was ridiculous. Burns was too pragmatic a politician to build his party only to subject it to a divisive primary battle. Richardson, for his part, would never run in a head-on election with Burns, whom he considered a political mentor.[10]

With formal announcement in March, 1966, of Richardson's nomination for the Chief Justice's slot, the press had a field day with his genealogy, misspelling names and mistaking relationships in its zeal. Although the articles never said so directly, they implied it was fitting that a part-Hawaiian head the judicial branch, a kind of vindication for the years of powerlessness inflicted upon native islanders. Only one other Hawaiian, Kauikeaouli—Kamehameha III—had held a similar position.

So the press made much of Richardson's Hawaiian-Chinese-*haole* lineage, pointing out that he was a product of the continuing migration process unique to the islands. He was also a product of a family with historic ties to the islands' judicial and legislative systems.

Hundreds of years ago, Richardson's Polynesian ancestors had travelled to the Sandwich Islands from the area around Tahiti. One of his forebears was Alapai-nui, chief of the Big Island during the 1700s and keeper of the war god Kuka-ilimoku.[11] A great great grandfather was Dubliner William Shaw, a cabin boy who jumped ship at Lahaina in 1807 when he was only fourteen years old. A great grandfather, English Captain John Richardson, was judge of the Second Circuit Court on Maui in 1848; he served also in the House of Representatives, the House of Nobles, and the Royal Privy Council. Captain Richardson's son, Colonel John Richardson, in large part repeated his father's career. The Hawaiian and *haole* bloodlines mixed through intermarriage. In time, Colonel Richardson's son and the future chief justice's father, Wilfred Kelelani Kanekoa Alapai, married Amy Lan Kyau Wung, the daughter of a Chinese immigrant family living in Kohala on the Big Island.[12] A more appropriate lineage could not be invented for a true son of the islands.

The public was told that Burns had two reasons for nominating Richardson for the Chief Justice's position. The first reason was his competence as an attorney. The second was the high esteem with which the Hawaii Bar regarded Richardson, as evidenced by his term as a past president of that body.

Insiders added a third reason. By appointing a part-Hawaiian to head one of the three co-equal branches of government, Burns would help dispel the feeling that Hawaiians could aspire only as high as the lieutenant governorship, a post which seemed reserved for them throughout the years.

This third reason provided continuing evidence of racial and ethnic tensions in the islands, no matter what the sugar-coated myths. It also underscored Democratic commitment to an ideal which fueled the peaceful revolution through the 1950s: limitless ceilings for qualified persons of all races. (Within the next few years, yet another reason for the appointment would become apparent. This fourth reason involved the high court's mandate to appoint trustees for the Bishop Estate, Princess Bernice Pauahi Bishop's legacy to her people. This complex fourth reason will be described in later pages.)

For the most part, the nomination and confirmation process went smoothly and expeditiously.

On a personal level, few could object to Richardson's selection. The adjectives used by reporters to describe him through the 1950s and early 1960s convey a demeanor unusual in its consistency: moderate, amiable, harmonizing. Furthermore, Richardson had established the reputation of being an efficient administrator, and administrative skill was an assumed requirement in any chief officer of the State courts. Through his work with the Democratic Party and his 1955–1957 assignment as Chief Clerk of the Senate, he had become familiar with the legislative process. And, of course, the lieutenant governorship had equipped him with first hand knowledge of the executive branch of government. A nominee with more balanced training in government would be hard to find.

Another crucial factor accounts for the quickness of Senate approval. By 1966, island Democrats were unquestionably ensconced in power and could do almost anything they wanted.

One after another, several witnesses at the hearing of the Senate Judiciary Committee spoke in high praise of Bill Richardson. Among them was Hung Wo Ching, then Aloha Airlines Board Chairman who had known Richardson since World War II as a friend and as an attorney: "I trust his integrity and judgment completely. Bill has always been a gentleman." Also among them was Masaji Marumoto, a former Supreme Court Justice who later would be reappointed to the Supreme Court bench. Although a staunch Republican, Marumoto was not perceived primarily as a political creature; his legal and judicial ability was unquestioned and seemed quite separate from his political leanings. Marumoto, as chairman of the Bar's judicial appointments committee, said that he was authorized to say the Hawaii State Bar Association felt Richardson was qualified for the post. He added: "I personally have no reservations about the nominee's ability."[13]

Only one person publicly questioned the appointment, an act which required courage—some said foolhardiness—given Richardson's obvious popularity and the inevitability of unanimous Senate approval.

Richard K. Sharpless, a former Territorial Attorney General and president of the Bar when Richardson was vice-president, brought into the open what was being stated quietly in some circles. The appointment, he declared, was purely political. To this, an observer harrumphed: Republican *or* Democrat, when was a gubernatorial appointment *ever* less than political? Another observer claimed that Sharpless' protest was tinged with envy since he had been reputed to be a candidate for the chief justice's position at one point.

Sharpless warned the Senate Judiciary Committee to proceed with caution. He stated that he had been a lawyer for thirty years and a Democrat for even longer. He declared he wanted to place some facts on the record and would feel compelled to do so even if the nominee were his own brother. Sharpless asserted that Richardson had been admitted to practice in 1946 on a motion before the Supreme Court; he had not taken and passed the exam usually required for admission to the Hawaii Bar. Furthermore, Sharpless said, he could not find any evidence that Richardson had ever argued a case before the Supreme Court.

When pressed by Senate Judiciary Committee chairman Sakae Takahashi, Sharpless would not say that Richardson was unqualified. Rather, he objected that the search for a new Chief Justice had not been more thorough and had not involved the Bar adequately enough. The appointment was not an end in itself but was a "pave-the-way" maneuver.[14]

Certainly, the appointment was not without political ramifications. Whoever filled the lieutenant governor's spot would be in direct line of succession to the top State post and would in likelihood be the Democratic contender for governor in 1970. Although a 1965 State succession law specified that the lieutenant governorship must be offered to the senate president in case of vacancy, public speculation was that Senate President Kazuhisa Abe would refuse it in preference to a future Supreme Court appointment.

Elmer Cravalho, the feisty and able House Speaker, was next in line. Political rumour was that Burns would like to "pave the way" for Cravalho to be his eventual successor. After a series of unsuccessful meetings between Burns and Cravalho, however, scuttlebutt had it that Cravalho was too independent and Burns too unwilling to detail an increased range of duties for the lieutenant governor's post. In the end, the lieutenant governorship would go to Andrew Ing, the State's Budget Director.

In any case, Sharpless was not very specific in voicing his reservations. His was a difficult position: how does one deal specifically and effectively with political rumours and one's own "feelings" about the aptness of a political appointment?

A valid concern was overlooked in the hubbub created by all the talk about political machinations. Masaji Marumoto had touched on this concern when he said in his testimony in support of Richardson: ". . . with respect to the judicial function, very frankly, there are some who have some qualms, since his legal qualifications have not been tested."[15]

This point most concerned some of Richardson's critics, especially those who were fellow members of the Bar. Displaying the caution normally attributed to their profession, they were unimpressed by news releases emanating from the Governor's Office which stated that Richardson had practiced law for seventeen years after receiving his degree from the University of Cincinnati. As to claims that Richardson had handled more than 1,000 cases in his career, the more suspicious detractors pointed out that there were cases and then there were cases—a collection agency case was not quite the same as a criminal case or one involving corporate matters.

Neither were his critics reassured by Gus Sproat, Chief Clerk of the Supreme Court, who said that Richardson and a handful of other young attorneys had been admitted to practice under wartime rules. Entering military service almost immediately after law school graduation, Richardson had begun his legal career in the Army Judge Advocate General Corps where he served from 1943 to 1946. He and other law school graduates who entered the armed forces directly after completion of law studies had been unable to return to the islands for the bar examination. Upon their return to Hawaii after serving in World War II, the exam had been waived for them; they instead supplied the court with character references and were sponsored by lawyers in good standing. The exam had been waived for a small number of lawyers including Marshall Goodsill, Jr., founding partner in a respected Honolulu law firm; William Fleming, president of the Hawaii Bar in 1966; John F. Dyer, a future Bar president and circuit judge; Norman K. Chung, also a future Bar president and the City's Corporation Counsel; and Suyeki

Okumura, a lawyer who would establish a reputation for legal and community leadership.[16]

So involved had Richardson been in politics after being admitted to the Bar that many of his legal colleagues did not know what kind of a lawyer he really was. They wondered if he could be elevated suddenly to the highest point in the judicial system and serve with any degree of distinction. But their concerns about Richardson's legal and judicial qualifications was buried in more pressing talk about political implications of the appointment.

Despite the rumblings of his critics—which in any event were neither loud, nor public, nor organized—Richardson breezed through the hearings to unanimous Senate approval.

The importance of the publicly-expressed opposition to Richardson's nomination lay not in its strength, which was minimal, but in the thrust of its major complaint. Critics through the years, over and over again, would raise questions about how past political ties affected the way Richardson discharged his judicial duties.

Thus, the rise of the Democratic Party through the late 1940s to the mid-1960s and Bill Richardson's reasons for involvement with the Party become indispensable backdrop to the periodic accusation that his politics impinged upon his judicial actions.

To come to any understanding of life in modern Hawaii, it is necessary to know the crucial role of partisan politics in its past. A basic question stirs continuing debate: to what degree was the Democratic Party responsible for toppling the old power elite and creating equal opportunity for all races? The answers vary, usually according to party affiliation and sometimes to the color of one's skin.

In the end, only four broad conclusions are acceptable to all persons involved in debate. First, World War II broke the historical insularity of the islands and, by bringing new wealth, new attitudes, and increased industrialization, provided a framework for change. Second, industrialization meant eventual unionization, and unionization increased the political strength of island workers, nearly all of whom joined the Democratic Party.[17] Third, the Democratic Party, activated by men whose vision was enlarged by wartime experiences and whose education often was subsidized by the GI Bill of Rights, played a part in changing the monolithic socio-economic and political structure in Hawaii. Fourth, partisan politics in its early days was ethnic politics and, although not as purely ethnic in more recent times, continues to be a vital force in the daily life of the islands.

Most accounts of the ascendancy of the Democratic Party in Hawaii somehow fail to tell the whole story.

The story's stark outline is simple enough.

In the 1954 elections, the *haole* Republican oligarchy began to give way—with some surprise—to a group of young island men mobilized by a Montana-born, but island-raised, farmer-turned-policeman, then liquor store owner and Civil Defense administrator. The reason for the surprise tells much about those Republicans: after more than half a century of dominance over island life, they felt invulnerable to the attacks of a small band of unknown, inexperienced non-*haole*s. Republicans grossly underestimated the group's ability to organize overwhelming numbers of island citizens into an electorate, most of it Japanese.[18]

Told simply in this way, the island story is commonplace. It echoes many similar stories in American history. After all, ethnic politics and exclusionary tactics practiced by the "haves" against the "have-nots" are natural in a nation peopled by successive waves of immigrants.

Yet, there is something extraordinary about the rise of the island Democratic Party which eludes description. No words can describe the intensity which fired the revolutionaries. No words, their primal need for ethnic and racial expression, recognition, and acceptance. Therefore, few accounts of those early years even begin to capture the emotions which consumed the Democrats and which propel many of them still. They talk today about that early battle against great odds, and they resort to hackneyed, inadequate phrases which frustrate them. They finally end with statements like "I still carry in my gut the anger I felt at the unfairness of island life in those days. If you weren't there, you *really* can't understand what our fight was all about."

A mystical bonding took place among those young men, many of whom had fought together during the Second World War to prove their allegiance to a doubting America. Their loyalty to one another would last for whole lifetimes, even through more modern times when such loyalty might seem unwise, outdated, or unfashionable. More than once, even the new breed of island Democrats would not understand this kind of unconditional loyalty; at times, even they would join other critics in dismissing it as cronyism or old-fashioned politics.

The men most responsible for bringing the Democratic Party to life quickly became a part of island political folklore. Like an ancient ritual chant, their names continue to be handed down from generation to generation, almost tedious in repetition. The earliest corps of men who joined Police Captain John Anthony Burns included those who came into contact with him through his wartime role as police liaison to the Japanese community; his Police Contact Group checked rumours, quieted scares, and mediated among various groups.

Dentist Ernest Murai and businessman Mitsuyuki Kido worked with the Contact Group, Kido as secretary of the AJA Emergency Service Committee, a body formed to demonstrate Japanese loyalty to America. Jack Kawano, a Japanese leader in the International Longshoremen's and Warehousemen's Union, was helpful in establishing ties between that group and the Democrat Party.

The litany of names continues. Daniel Aoki, an early president of the AJA 442nd veteran group, reluctantly was persuaded that votes of his regiment and of his race could overturn the established order of things in Hawaii; once committed, Aoki remained as an aide to Burns throughout his years in public office. Mike Tokunaga was influenced by his father, a plantation *luna* or foreman, into angry perception of the inequities in plantation life; he joined the growing nucleus as one of its more activist members.

Others among the group translated their idealism into community involvement as the years passed; they became doers, policy makers, and opinion molders through their high public positions. Daniel Inouye, an extremely important catalyst among the early workers, later became the first AJA elected to the U.S. House of Representatives, then to the Senate. Sakae Takahashi, a member of the AJA 100th Battalion, in time became Territorial Treasurer, and Michiro Watanabe became the Attorney General; they were the first *nisei,* or second generation Japanese, to be named to top island posts. Takahashi later moved on to assume the job of majority leader of the State Senate. Masato Doi, a respected circuit court judge, eventually lost his bid for the post of mayor of the City and County of Honolulu in spite of a well-organized campaign. Herman Lum became U.S. Attorney, then family court judge, then an associate justice of the State Supreme Court.[19] Matsuo Takabuki was elected to the City and County's Board of Supervisors, then to the City Council after Statehood; his later appointment as trustee of Princess Bernice Pauahi Bishop's legacy would be highly controversial. Robert Oshiro, attorney, established a legendary reputation as a political campaign organizer.[20]

Bill Richardson channeled his energies into party building and marshalling Hawaiian votes to work in tandem with Japanese votes; it seemed an unlikely beginning for a future chief justice.

In Richardson's case, the feeling of injustice which spurred the other young Democrats was a little more complicated. As a member of a minority in ethnic and political terms, he felt the same social, economic and political deprivations. In addition, as a native Hawaiian—as descendant of an Hawaiian chief and inheritor of familial allegiance to the monarchy—he carried an ancient memory of dispossession in his bones. That memory was rekindled among his people with the birth of every new generation; the imperative to regain possession of their lands and their government remained a strong undercurrent in their culture.

Even in his childhood years, Richardson had absorbed the lesson that politics could be the vehicle for changes beneficial to Hawaiians. His paternal grandmother was an active Democrat on Maui at a time when it was neither popular nor especially wise to be one. Mary Ann Kaulaikalauele Shaw Richardson—the same Kaula Shaw who used to be confined to the upper alcove in Iolani Palace for childish misdeeds—instilled in her son Wilfred a devotion to the Democratic and Hawaiian causes, which she viewed as intertwined. Her husband, Colonel John Richardson, Queen Liliuokalani's legal representative in Washington, D.C retained his royalist sentiments for all of his life. In fact, they seemed to grow stronger with the passing of time; crippled in his old age, his railings against the white displacers grew more strident and insistent.

Wilfred, Bill Richardson's father, was the only one of his siblings to become a Democrat; the others, like many Hawaiians including Prince Kuhio, found it more sensible to work for their cause through the all-powerful Republican Party. In his later years, Wilfred Richardson was fond of describing himself as a "one-time struggling politician." Of his various experiences, he cherished politics most. Family illness had kept him from the kind of education which would allow him to follow in his father's and grandfather's legal footsteps. He worked at a number of occupations, including operating his own business as a bail bondsman. Whatever his job, political activity was his avocation. Citing his bondsman's experience with money matters, he twice ran unsuccessfully for the job of City treasurer. His office on Nuuanu Street was a gathering place for the pre-war Democratic warhorses—Johnny Wilson, David Trask, Manuel Pacheco, Bill Heen, Noble Kauhane.

Under the tutelage of family and politically-inclined friends, Bill Richardson saw that the tide which had shifted the balance of power away from Hawaiians needed to be stemmed. The advice articulated by Johnny Wilson, son of the Queen's marshal and himself Mayor of Honolulu from 1920–26, 1929–30, and 1947–1954, summarized Richardson's early political lessons: "Bill, you've got to do things for the Hawaiian people; you've got to work for them. Politics is the way to do it."

The lessons of one's formative years are not easily forgotten.

Richardson knew that in his new position as Chief Justice he must develop and display traits normally imputed to a judicial personality. During the Throne Room ceremony which commissioned him as Chief Justice, Richardson publicly severed ties with his party. He thanked Democrats for their past loyalty, acknowledged that he could no longer be a "foot soldier" in the Party, and assured all citizens—Democrats and Republicans alike—that he would value their support and serve their interests.

Nevertheless, it became obvious as years passed that Richardson believed a man did not "resign from the human race" just because he became Chief Justice.[21] He refused to disown past friendships or to disclaim his own people's history or to disavow completely his personal and political philosophy. In Bill Richardson's case—as in the case of many other early island Democrats who rose to positions of community leadership—the Democratic Party had fomented a liberal philosophy which transcended the limits of partisan politics. It also had encouraged in Richardson a proclivity toward activism as a means to correct imbalances he saw in his island community. Lastly, fighting for the Democratic cause had instilled in him a strong, unquestioning loyalty to those who fought beside him.

Those lessons would stay with him even after he left the political arena for the ostensibly more temperate, dispassionate world of judicial concerns.

---

1. *Honolulu Advertiser,* Gene Hunter, Feb. 26, 1966.

2. The word *haole* initially referred to any foreigner; in time it specifically referred to a Caucasian usually of American or English extraction.

3. *Honolulu Advertiser,* Drew McKillips, March 26, 1966.

4. *Ibid.*

5. *Honolulu Advertiser,* March 26, 1966.

6. *Honolulu Star-Bulletin,* March 26, 1966. The high regard with which the press treated Richardson seems unusual, even in a day when the island community was smaller, possibly more imbued with the "Spirit of Aloha," and relationships tended to be more personalized. Political analyst Dan F. Tuttle, Jr., described Richardson's popularity with voters and wrote that his departure from the Democratic ticket "could prove more damaging than many calculate." *Honolulu Advertiser,* Jan. 2, 1966. Veteran *Star-Bulletin* political writer Douglas Boswell commented in a March 16, 1966 article on Richardson's reputation, remarkably "unbesmirched" after fifteen years in politics.

7. However, as early as 1959, the press independently had speculated on

the possibility that Richardson might one day be named chief justice. *Honolulu Star-Bulletin,* Sam Frear, May 31, 1959.

8. *Honolulu Star-Bulletin,* Tomi Knaefler, Feb. 25, 1966. (Slight modification of quote for readability.)

9. *Honolulu Star-Bulletin,* May 14, 1956.

10. Statement of William S. Richardson, in a personal interview, Honolulu, Hawaii, Dec. 17, 1981.

11. Kuka-ilimoku was the most well-known of war gods owned by Kamehameha; to be entrusted with its care was high honor.

12. Amy Ching Richardson spent twenty years compiling the Richardson geneaology, a detailed document containing information gleaned from the Archives of Hawaii, visits to gravesites, and numerous conversations with old Hawaiians.

13. *Honolulu Star-Bulletin,* March 15, 1966. Others who gave favorable testimony included attorney Thomas Flynn, vice-president of the Bar when Richardson was president; Dr. George Mills, president of the Hawaiian Civic Clubs; Harry Albright, retired military officer and a Richardson colleague in the Honolulu chapter of the Reserve Officers Association; and Senator David K. Trask.

14. *Honolulu Star-Bulletin,* March 15, 1966, articles including one bylined by Douglas Boswell.

15. *Honolulu Star-Bulletin,* March 15, 1966.

16. From files of the Office of the Supreme Court Chief Clerk, courtesy of Samuel K. Makekau. A total of ten lawyers were admitted to the Bar in accordance with the Amendment to Paragraph 3 of Rule 15 adopted by the Supreme Court on Jan. 5, 1942.

17. The unions played an important part in the political overthrow of the *status quo* in the islands. For instance, in 1962 they took the term "Big Five" which historically had referred to the powerful economic conglomerates—American Factors, Alexander and Baldwin, C. Brewer and Co., Castle and Cooke, Theo. H. Davies and Co., Ltd.—and they used the term to describe union endorsement of five major Democratic candidates. Endorsed early in the various 1962 campaigns were John Burns for governor, Ernest Kai for lieutenant governor, Daniel Inouye for U.S. Senate, Tom Gill and "Spark" Matsunaga for the U.S. House. It was only after Richardson defeated Kai in the Democratic primary that he won union support as one of the "Big Five."

18. In 1964 and 1966, University of Hawaii professor Daniel W. Tuttle, Jr., compiled information on voting statistics from official election data and on voter characteristics from official census reports. With this

information as a base, a pattern of voting behavior emerges confirming inferences made by an earlier Tuttle study (with John M. Digman) about ethnic composition of the two political parties. Without doubt, the Japanese began to use the Democratic Party as their vehicle for political expression from the early 1950s, even though many of them officially proclaimed themselves "Independents" in their early grasp for power. Daniel W. Tuttle, Jr., *Hawaii Voting Behavior: A Background Guide to Some Significant Characteristics of Honolulu's (Oahu's) 138 Precincts* (Honolulu: University of Hawaii Department of Political Science, 1965); Daniel W. Tuttle, Jr., *Hawaii Voting Behavior: A Background Guide to Some Significant Characteristics of Honolulu's (Oahu's) 141 Precincts* (Honolulu: [n.n.], 1968).

Although 1954 was the year that the dramatic revolution took place at the polls, starting from the 1920s, a few Japanese dissidents had been at work, encouraging their fellow immigrants toward activism. For example, Yasutaro Soga of the *Nippu Jiji* and Fred Makino of the *Hawaii Hochi* used their newspapers to encourage labor strikes. Makino was the more militant, constantly urging Japanese to win social and political equality through politics.

19. Lum would succeed Richardson as Chief Justice, being sworn into the post on April 26, 1983.

20. Oshiro, in fact, choreographed the ceremonies which ushered Richardson in as Chief Justice.

21. *Honolulu Star Bulletin,* Byron Baker, Aug. 1, 1968.

Photo Identification
Chapter I, p. x
William Shaw Richardson, center, with parents Amy and Wilfred Richardson on "boat day" as he leaves for the mainland and law school in 1941.

"You nominate a chief justice because the two of you share a common philosophy. When I say 'common philosophy', I do not refer to mere partisanship, although some degree of partisanship may be inevitable in any judicial appointment."

John Anthony Burns, Governor, State of Hawaii
August 1, 1968[1]

II
The Judicial and Executive Relationship

Judicial robes offered the new Chief Justice very little protection from being drawn into the 1966 gubernatorial campaign.

At summer's end, Republican candidate Randolph Crossley made much of a Friday lunch tradition started by Burns many years earlier. The luncheon group's basic nucleus consisted of a handful of regulars: T. G. S. Walker, Kahuku Sugar Plantation manager whose liberal views set him apart from other managers; Edward Burns, the Governor's brother who in time would be gubernatorially-appointed head of the Department of Taxation; Lewers and Cooke executive R. Gibson Rietow. Richardson, Aloha Airlines executive Hung Wo Ching, and stevedoring company leader Thomas J. McCabe became part of the luncheon group some time after its inception.[2]

Crossley accused Burns and Richardson of a breach of ethics in continuing the lunch tradition for so many years. Among Crossley's concerns was that the weekly lunches encouraged the executive and judicial branches to be too "chummy."

Burns' style was to ignore such comments.

Richardson retorted: "I've been having lunch each Friday with my friends for fifteen years. I see no reason to stop that tradition now."

Crossley's comments reached a head in 1968, two years after he lost a hard-fought battle for the governorship. Replete with political overtones, a lawsuit filed by the Republican Party was docketed for the State Supreme Court early that year. The suit claimed that the ballots were improperly designed and that there were vote-tallying irregularities. Republican Crossley and his running mate George H. Mills disagreed with the lower court ruling that the ballots and their tallying procedures were valid. With the Republican Party, they appealed the case and moved that three of the justices then sitting on the Supreme Court bench disqualify themselves. Gubernatorially-appointed as they were, their positions would be affected by the outcome of the case, the plaintiffs claimed.

Before the motion progressed very far, Associate Justices Kazuhisa Abe, Bernard H. Levinson, and Masaji Marumoto removed themselves from hearing the case, with no comment about the issues raised. Associate Justice Jack Mizuha was not named in the Crossley-Mills motion because he had been the last court appointment of the previous governor, Republican William F. Quinn; also, he had indicated that he would retire in June, 1968.

Crossley then filed an action in the Supreme Court requesting that the Chief Justice remove himself from the case because he and the governor not only lunched together every Friday but frequently breakfasted together, a sure sign—he said—that the judicial and executive branches were too close.

Richardson refused to disqualify himself.

Even those who saw validity in Crossley's charges were hard pressed to see where he was headed. Political wags asked: Will circuit court judges fill in at the Supreme Court level, but only long enough to disqualify themselves because they too are appointees of this Democratic administration?[3]

Crossley, an interesting figure in island politics, had arrived from the mainland United States to build a reputation as a shrewd businessman through the 1930s. In short order, he was elected to represent the island of Kauai in the legislature, then to chair the Republican Party. Whatever his personality traits may have been as a young man, he was not a sympathetic figure as an older man. A testy and crotchety candidate who muted these traits through most of the 1966 gubernatorial campaign, he revealed himself unfavorably as he wended his way through the lawsuit in 1967 and 1968. Perhaps Crossley's petulance sprang in part from remembrance of the governorship which he felt was capriciously denied him in 1954, when President Dwight D. Eisenhower unexpectedly named the part-Hawaiian Samuel Wilder King governor of Hawaii.[4] Whatever the reason, any merit in charges made by Crossley and the Republican Party was obscured as a certain pettiness emerged and pervaded the whole lawsuit incident.

Finally in June of 1968, a unanimous Supreme Court decision confirmed that Jack Burns and Tom Gill were indeed Hawaii's governor and lieutenant governor. The Crossley-Mills charges which arose specifically out of the 1966 balloting were put to rest. But other charges of politicization continued and came not only from Republicans. The appearance of executive and judicial "chumminess" was strong enough to offend even some Democrats, many of them younger and strangers to the early Party search for identity and power.

Delegates to the 1968 Constitutional Convention debated methods of judicial selection, hearing conflicting testimony from all sides. The Bar Association had one proposal. A group called the "Citizens Administration of Justice Foundation" had some suggestions.[5] Defenders of the *status quo* had their own ideas: gubernatorial appointment with Senate approval of Supreme Court and circuit judges was tested and true. Why change anything?

C. Frank Damon, then president of the Bar, spoke on behalf of his organization. His call for higher salary for judges, longer tenure, an attractive pension, and selection and retention based on merit hardly seemed controversial. Yet, in detailing his suggestions, Damon aroused strong reactions. The Bar suggested a non-partisan judicial selection commission composed of both lawyers and laymen: such a commission would promote active search for judicial talent. The Bar's inference was clear—gubernatorial appointment did not involve wide, thorough search for the best available judicial talent.

Attorney General Bert Kobayashi, Sr., whom Burns often referred to as the "strong right arm of this administration,"[6] spoke against change. Delegate John Dyer, a former circuit judge not reappointed by Burns, asked him why he took that position. Kobayashi, a direct and pragmatic man, answered: "The Governor prefers the present system." Besides, he added, some degree of politics, some feeling of philosophical kinship, inevitably characterizes any appointment. To give appointing authority to a commission merely diffused the chances that politics would influence judicial selection.

Kobayashi's next statement released a hornet's nest. Sure, in Hawaii—as everywhere else—politics entered into the appointment process, he said. But here, the politics was "good, clean."[7]

The natural reaction to that statement followed in an instant.

Young Democrat Nelson Doi from the Big Island asked: "Just what is your definition of 'good politics'? How would you differentiate 'good politics' from 'bad politics'?"

Then, bluntly and emotionally, as was his wont, Doi demanded: "Don't you think the appointment by the Governor of Richardson as chief justice did violence to the separation of powers doctrine and to his [Richardson's] mandate from the people as lieutenant governor?"[8]

Kobayashi spoke about how Richardson's appointment was politically detrimental to Burns, for the two men had "tremendous rapport." Burns let Richardson go because he believed that he had the necessary qualities and credentials for the post, Kobayashi asserted.[9]

Kobayashi was joined by other *status quo* proponents who set forth convincing arguments. They pointed out that the State Bar itself was not unanimously convinced of the desirability of what was called the "Bar Plan." Also, there seemed to be inherent factional conflict within the Bar between attorneys of large firms and small firms, plaintiff attorneys and defendant attorneys. Moreover, what accountability would commissioners have to the electorate? Wouldn't politics enter into commission deliberations and final appointments? Couldn't one faction of the commission become so steeped in power that it would become totally unresponsive to the people?[10]

Many proponents of the *status quo* were, ironically, the same persons who had pressed for revolutionary changes in the 1950s. Then, with good reason, they had protested Presidential appointment of island judges, believing that the power of judicial appointment should be somehow closer to the people whom judges served. In 1968, they believed that vesting authority for judicial appointments in the governor was fair and acceptable. By 1968, the power of those early Party-building Democrats was unchallengeable, and the move to dilute gubernatorial authority for judicial appointments sputtered along disjointedly.

A Constitutional Convention vote put the issue to rest, and the dissident voices were temporarily silenced.

The respite was brief.

Within three years, charges would arise once more that ties between the State's executive and judicial branches were much too close.

Early in the summer of 1971, the Supreme Court of Hawaii—as prescribed by Princess Bernice Pauahi Bishop's will since 1883—announced a new appointment to the Bishop Estate board of trustees. Matsuo Takabuki, a Burns-Richardson ally for more than twenty years, was named to fill a vacancy created by the death of Herbert K. Keppeler.

The five-man board was led in mid-1971 by part-Hawaiian Richard Lyman. Other members were *haole* Frank Midkiff and part-Hawaiian Edwin Murray. The fourth, most-recently named trustee was Hung Wo Ching. Ching's appointment in 1968 had broken the tradition of a board racially composed of a predominance of *haole*s and a sprinkling of part-Hawaiians.[11]

Mrs. Bishop, a lineal descendant of King Kamehameha I, had left nearly all her property in trust to establish two schools, one for boys, the other for girls. To the lands inherited from her parents, royal councillor Abner Paki and Kamehameha I's granddaughter Konia, Mrs. Bishop had added lands of the Kamehameha family upon the death of her cousin, Princess Ruth Keelikolani. Upon her own death a year later, Mrs. Bishop stated through her will that income from these lands was to be used for educational purposes for the "children of Hawaii." Her will did not define specifically the term "children of Hawaii," but the first board of trustees, which included Mrs. Bishop's husband, Charles, established a policy limiting enrollment to children of Hawaiian and part-Hawaiian ancestry.

In addition, Mrs. Bishop's will did not define specifically the curricula for the Kamehameha Schools. The will called "first and chiefly" for "a good education in the common English branches and also instruction in morals and in such useful knowledge as may tend to make industrious men and women." Mrs. Bishop did indicate some priority among possible school courses when she added in her will: "I desire instruction in the higher branches to be subsidiary to the foregoing objects."[12]

Again, the first board of trustees interpreted and implemented what it understood to be the general intent of Mrs. Bishop's will. Over the years, ensuing boards continued to place curricular emphasis on the industrial and vocational arts, causing some people to deplore the paternalism evident in such philosophical interpretation and practical application of Mrs. Bishop's will.

Bill Richardson's parents were among those who believed that the Kamehameha Schools deprived students of strong academic training. This belief, plus their inability to pay even the minimal fees charged by the Schools, had accounted for their children's attendance at public schools.[13] They had decided that their youngsters had more access to college-preparatory training in the public school system, in spite of what they perceived as the same kind of paternalism at work in that system.

After he became Chief Justice, Bill Richardson made no secret of his feelings that the Bishop Estate trustees needed to correct two deficiencies created by past board biases, limitations, and shortsightedness. First, the Estate must generate more income and provide higher financial indices of successful business management. Second, the Estate must reexamine the will's intent and encourage relevant, academic curricula in order to serve more purposively the legatees of Mrs. Bishop's will.[14]

Richardson and his court intended to address the first of these deficiencies with lawyer-businessman Takabuki's appointment, but the appointment met with great public outcry and condemnation.

Governor Burns had manipulated the appointment, objectors said, thereby repaying political services rendered by Takabuki. Close ties between Burns and Richardson and Takabuki had allowed this kind of manipulation, they argued, manipulation which was a disservice to the entire community and the Hawaiian community in particular. In fact, some objectors continued, Burns had appointed Richardson as Chief Justice with future Bishop Estate appointments in mind. The public long knew that the Governor felt a bond with native Hawaiians, his personal anger at social injustice extending to all peoples who were displaced or dispossessed.[15]

Some of the arguments contradicted each other. Those with any kind of interest in island sociology knew that for some reason the Hawaiian and Japanese races were historically antagonistic to each other.[16] If the Governor sought to control trustee appointments in the interests of Hawaiians, why would he appoint anyone, especially a Japanese, who would not serve those interests well?

The importance of a trusteeship lay in a number of factors. Bishop Estate always had been more than a unique, tax-free educational institution. With its 344,000 acres, one-ninth of the islands' total land area, the Estate was also Hawaii's largest and wealthiest private landowner. By virtue of limited space and a growing population, the Estate would become purveyor of an increasingly precious commodity: its real worth in 1970 was estimated at $400 million.

In 1970, trustees earned approximately $50,000 in annual commissions from Estate lands. The sum, while healthy, was scarce enticement for a candidate to sever conflict-of-interest ties in law, business, or real estate. Thus, the public clamor may have seemed the proverbial tempest in a teapot to some, but others knew that the appointment as trustee was not only prestigious, challenging, but potentially lucrative. Indeed, within a decade, each trustee would be earning more than $180,000 a year.

The first issue of the "Honolulu News," a political tabloid listing Democrat mayor Frank Fasi as editor, described the dark motives and dire consequences of Takabuki's appointment. The article drew sinister relationships among several groups: the Burns machine; the justices of Hawaii's Supreme Court; news publisher and financier Chinn Ho (for whom Takabuki worked as "political muscleman" before becoming vice-president of Ho's Capital Investment Co.); and various other businessmen. The article asserted that Takabuki was named trustee so he could use that position for the benefit of "political cronies," not the Hawaiian people.[17]

Interestingly, Takabuki's appointment pitted distaff members of the Richardson family against the Chief Justice. In a show of steadfast male solidarity and out of deference to their brother, the first-born son, the Richardson men took no part in the family argument.

Even years after the furor, Bill Richardson said he did not know the feelings any of his brothers or brothers-in-law had about Takabuki's appointment, adding, "If my father had been alive, I believe he also would have kept silent about his feelings."

But Pearl, the youngest sister and second youngest of the siblings, felt no such compunctions about silence. She made her feelings known in no uncertain terms, joining protestors as they marched with placards around King Kamehameha's statue in front of the judiciary building.

The eldest Richardson child, Amy, lived in New Mexico with her family, in charge of the Pilialoha Motel, established by her parents in 1947 and run by them for the next ten years. Amy was geographically beyond Pearl's reach, but

Pearl convinced Grace—the next eldest child, two years older than the Chief Justice—to join her in a visit to their brother's chambers. The visit was marked by cool cordiality and no relenting of either side.

Arlon, two years younger than the Chief Justice, was unable to keep his wife Mary from succumbing to Pearl's recruitment.

Ever the activist, Pearl then wooed Helen, wife of the youngest Richardson, Bobby, into her camp.

When the bell at Kawaiahao Church tolled in objection to Takabuki's appointment, Pearl prevailed upon Mary to telephone the Chief Justice.

"Brother-in-law," Mary said. "Do you hear the bell? Do you realize *you* are responsible for the ringing of the bell?"

To this the Chief Justice replied, "Sister-in-law, the appointment is a unanimous decision of the Supreme Court, not my decision alone. Besides that, I believe that the appointment is a good one."

Abraham Akaka, minister of Kawaiahao Church, the first church organized by the Boston missionaries to the islands, had issued a dramatically-worded statement about the ringing of the Church bell. He said that the bell, joined by other church bells throughout the island chain, protested the oppression of the Hawaiian race, oppression which he hinted was continued with the naming of a Japanese trustee.

Some persons observed snidely that Akaka's statement tasted of sour grapes, since he himself wanted the appointment as trustee.

Even an *Advertiser* editorial questioned Akaka's motives and behavior. Akaka had gained favorable national attention with sermons extolling the exemplary brotherhood of races in Hawaii. He had likened the several island races to the strings of an ukulele. Truly, individually tuned, the strings produced a beautiful and unparalleled harmony, he said. And all of the strings were necessary for the songs they produced.

What has happened to the Reverend Akaka's famed ukulele?, the editorial asked.[18]

Mother Amy Wung Richardson sent a letter to her son objecting to the appointment. Her letter echoed much of what the Hawaiian community was saying: What could a Japanese possibly know about a Hawaiian, especially about what kind of education was best for a Hawaiian? Was there no qualified Hawaiian to be named trustee of a legacy intended for children of his own race?

The Chief Justice telephoned his mother, asking why suddenly she was objecting to an appointment on the apparent basis of race. Why had she not voiced this kind of concern when the Chinese Hung Wo Ching had been named Bishop Estate trustee two years earlier? Well, she answered, she had not liked *that* appointment much either.

The child stood firm, reminding his mother that it was she who had taught him not to yield once he took a stand which he believed was right.

"I wish you would set your daughters straight," he said to his mother.

Although he could never know for sure, the Chief Justice believed that after this conversation, his mother prevailed upon her daughters in individual conversations to ease their pressure upon their brother.

A circus-like air began to permeate the entire affair, with spokespersons appearing at every corner. It was difficult to tell where sincerity left off and grandstanding began.

Art Rutledge, the peripatetic Unity House union organizer, made a suggestion as Hawaiians continued their protests against the Japanese appointee: "All they have to do is get Mr. Takabuki and Chief Justice Richardson to trade places. Then everybody would be happy."[19]

Somone pointed to a provision in Mrs. Bishop's will specifying that trustees be Protestant: Mr. Takabuki might not meet that requirement. This suggestion drew the Reverend Hiro Higuchi, chaplain of the 442nd Battalion, into the fray. He attested that Takabuki frequently attended Protestant services while overseas.[20]

Meanwhile, the marching continued in front of the Judiciary building. A small contingent of demonstrators also was deployed to the Bishop Estate office a few blocks away on Halekauwila Street. When labor leader Walter Kupau endorsed Takabuki's appointment, yet another band was deployed to picket offices of the AFL-CIO Hawaii State Federation of Labor.

The words of Masaji Marumoto, now an associate justice, once again had a quietening effect, if only for a short while. In an act which was noted by the press as unusual, Marumoto released a written statement describing the High Court procedure which had resulted in Takabuki's appointment. Marumoto said that when the vacancy occurred, the justices made a study of all possible applicants, including those who had not applied for the post.

Afterwards, upon examination of candidate lists turned in by each justice, Marumoto noted that "A remarkable feature . . . was that no name on any justice's list was duplicated on another justice's list, thus showing clearly that there was no outside influence exerted on a group of justices."

In the event that any one mistake his meaning, Marumoto said even more explicitly, "(I)n the four years that I have served on the bench after being appointed by Governor Burns in May, 1967, I have yet to see an instance where the Governor made even an attempt to influence or interfere with prerogatives of the judiciary."[21]

When Marumoto released his statement, the Chief Justice was away at a meeting in Charleston, S.C. When he returned, he spoke with a reporter, stressing that Marumoto's was a personal statement and not one made for or by the entire court. He indicated, however, that he personally agreed with Marumoto's comments. He said that in addition to names submitted for the present slot, Supreme Court justices also had reviewed the more than sixty names earlier suggested for the 1968 vacancy. He confirmed Marumoto's statement that there was no repetition of any names when the justices submitted their individual lists of nominees. He added, in an aside, that he knew which justice had nominated Takabuki, for he had recognized his handwriting.[22]

A parade seemed appropriate at this point, especially in a state whose people traditionally love such displays, and whose weather encourages such outdoor events.

Politicians and other public figures marched with a thousand protestors down Waikiki's Kalakaua Avenue to Kapiolani Park, some out of real conviction, others, because they were ever alert to the possibilities of good press through identification with a popular cause. They were joined at the Park by hundreds of other protestors, and they listened to several speakers including the Reverend Akaka; Colonel Curtis Kekoa, chairman of the "Ad Hoc Committee for a Hawaiian Trustee"; and Pae Galdeira, leader of a group called plainly, "The Hawaiians."

Then, one by one, they addressed the crowd. Mayor Fasi spoke, as did part-Hawaiian attorney Samuel P. King, son of a former governor and himself a 1970 Republican candidate for governor. Former lieutenant governor Thomas P. Gill also spoke: the long-standing wary, prickly relationship between Burns and Gill had disintegrated completely by then, underscored by Burns' preference for part-Hawaiian businessman Kenny Brown as running mate during the 1966 gubernatorial campaign. The personal and political barriers between Fasi, King, and Gill dissolved temporarily in their united stand against Takabuki's appointment.[23]

The emotions of the moment overshadowed a few telling and provocative thoughts which were expressed as the incident ran its course. One of these came from the Reverend Darrow Aiona. His was not a necessarily logical statement, but it eloquently revealed a certain logic of the heart: "If the purpose of the Bishop Estate is to educate the Hawaiian people, then the appointment of a non-Hawaiian must mean . . . that no Hawaiian is competent. If this is correct, then seventy years of domination of the Estate by non-Hawaiians shows that the trustees have failed in their duty in carrying out Princess Pauahi's will."[24]

The Reverend Charles Crane quietly made another important observation. He suggested that the outcry had nothing to do with racism. It was simply "another eruption of the discomfort, frustration and hostility that surrounds the whole administration of Princess Pauahi's will." Pointing out that nineteenth-century benevolence did not match twentieth-century problems, Crane said he wept at the incongruity of the tremendous assets of the Bishop Estate "going to support a private school for a limited number of exclusively selected children."[25]

An editorial in the *Honolulu Star-Bulletin* had commented earlier along the same lines: "It would bring tears to Mrs. Bishop's eyes to see how many Hawaiian-blooded children have not become 'industrious men and women' but strangers in their own homeland, providing an unhappily high proportion of its negative social statistics."[26]

Takabuki's investiture as trustee took place on July 30, 1971, in spite of the protests, in spite of the tolling of the bells.[27] He worked quietly for the next several months, even in the face of continued rumblings.

When he made his first public appearance in February of the next year, he addressed the annual convention of the State Association of Hawaiian Civic Clubs. He talked about the trustees' work and the future plans the Board had for the Estate and the beneficiaries of the Estate. He also spoke about his appointment, the first formal public statement in his own defense. He called for a balance between ethnic identity and the "concept of blending," asking his audience not to discount the efforts of "outsiders." He continued somewhat melodramatically: "When does the search for ethnic identity become divisive? Is Abraham Lincoln irrelevant to Blacks because he was not one of them?"[28]

At the end of his speech, the audience rose in ovation.

Whatever the response of the Hawaiian Civic Clubs in February, 1972, a suit to keep Takabuki from the trusteeship had been filed early in July, 1971, a suit which continued to be pressed through the early months of 1974.

Filed on behalf of several parties including twelve-year old Kevin James Kekoa, son of Col. Kekoa, chairman of the Ad Hoc Committee for a Hawaiian Trustee, the case was heard by circuit judge Yasutaka Fukushima.

Judge Fukushima held that the plaintiffs had no right to intervene in Takabuki's appointment and that he, as circuit judge, had no authority to review and rule on the actions of Supreme Court justices.

Dissatisfied with Fukushima's conclusions, the plaintiffs then took their case to the State Supreme Court.

In an unprecedented but ethically necessary move, all five Supreme Court justices who had appointed Takabuki removed themselves from hearing the case.[29] They then asked attorney Walter G. Chuck to represent them. The Chief Justice appointed replacements from among the circuit judges. Circuit judge Allen R. Hawkins, the longest tenured judge, became Acting Chief Justice of the newly formed temporary court. Thomas S. Ogata sat in for Masaji Marumoto; Alfred Laureta for Kazuhisa Abe; Herman T. F. Lum for Bernard H. Levinson; John C. Lanham for Bert. T. Kobayashi, Sr.

Showing some originality and a certain disregard for Mrs.

Bishop's will, a battery of attorneys led by Samuel P. King, Thomas P. Gill, and Arthur K. Trask alleged that the Takabuki appointment violated the code of judicial ethics.[30] They claimed that the Bishop Estate, as a "quasi-public" entity, had denied Estate beneficiaries due process of law; beneficiaries had been given neither advance notice of the appointment nor an opportunity to be heard. They sought to change the Princess' will by devising a new method of naming Estate trustees which would involve interested citizens.

Bishop Estate trustees were represented by J. Garner Anthony, who claimed that Mrs. Bishop's will was "perfectly clear and unambiguous" in giving High Court justices the authority to appoint trustees.[31] Anthony said that the plaintiffs had no standing in court; only the State's Attorney General, not the plaintiffs, had the right to come to court to enforce a charitable trust.

The State's Attorney General claimed that if Bishop Estate lands were indeed "quasi-public," then the Kamehameha Schools should adhere to hiring and admission policies laid down for all public institutions. Even the most zealous of the plaintiffs did not wish to win the suit if it meant that students of Hawaiian ancestry might not have continued sole access to benefits from the Estate.

The substitute Supreme Court supported the legitimacy of Takabuki's appointment.

Doggedly, the plaintiffs appealed to the U.S. Supreme Court, claiming that because State Supreme Court justices had named Takabuki to his post, that constituted "state action" and was therefore subject to the U.S. constitutional guarantee of due process.

With refusal of the U.S. Supreme Court to intervene, plaintiffs had exhausted every legal recourse and the matter came to an end.

Richardson, years later, continued to defend his frequent meetings with the Governor, claiming that the relationship contained no untoward influence of one branch of government over the other.

"Of course, we talked about the Judiciary, but only about the administrative design and the administrative needs of the system, never about substantive law before cases were heard or as they were in progress. I would be foolish, and negligent in my duties as administrator of the courts, if I didn't let the Governor and the legislature know how much money I needed, what kind of personnel I needed, what kind of buildings I needed."

"I remember that the Governor used to have a lot of gripes about some of the law that came out of the Judiciary. I told him to stay on his side of the fence."

As for the Friday lunch group, Richardson continued to insist that it was a bi-partisan group, "political" only in the sense that ideas which later became reality were presented at first in the confidential setting of the group.

"Take the beefing up of the University of Hawaii, and especially of the athletic department there. Long before the first public mention of buildup plans for the University, the Friday group held serious discussions about people who should be approached for help, about alternative methods of reaching the goal, about fallback plans. *Those* were the kinds of things we discussed at the Friday lunches."

Richardson also saw the luncheons as a way to keep in touch with the community. "You can't be a judge, sit in your own bailiwick and not know what's going on outside the Judiciary. A judge has to make a determined effort to reach out to people, to keep in touch with various constituencies."

On the question of gubernatorial appointment of judges, Richardson continued to agree with *status quo* proponents in the 1968 Constitutional Convention. During the State

Constitutional Convention held a decade later, the Chief Justice would present testimony against the formation of a judicial selection commission, believing that such action merely increased the points at which politics could become part of the selection process. Convention delegates in 1978 would disagree with this point of view and approve an adaptation of the 1968 "Bar Plan." As opposed as he was to that plan or any offshoot thereof, with electorate approval of a judicial selection commission of nine members variously appointed and elected, the Chief Justice began to see strengths of the commission-system and eventually accepted it as a satisfactory means of judicial selection.[32]

As for the educational legacy of the islands, Richardson continued to believe that island youngsters, especially those at Kamehameha Schools, suffered because educational policy was decided for too many years by those who felt non-*haole*s were "genetically inferior" and who wished to relegate these peoples to subordinate roles.[33]

The Chief Justice continued to profess no regrets about Takabuki's appointment or the earlier 1968 appointment of Hung Wo Ching, even when competitive friction developed over the years between Takabuki and Ching.[34]

Admitting that a reason the Takabuki appointment pleased him was that "Matsy" was a Burns-Richardson ally, the Chief Justice asserted that the meaning of the appointment went far beyond the simple pleasure of being able to name a trusted, competent, longtime friend to an important post.

"One meaning of the Takabuki appointment was that it reinforced the symbolic statement that the Supreme Court had made earlier with its appointment of Hung Wo Ching: it challenged the island mentality which held that only *haole*s and a few part-Hawaiians could serve the Princess as trustee of her estate.

"And by appointing non-*haole*s and non-Hawaiians of

such obvious ability, the Court could never be accused of appointing a token Japanese or a token Chinese just so it could move beyond the confines of tradition.

"Another meaning of the Takabuki appointment—and the earlier Ching appointment—was that both men would bring their business training and acumen to the management of Bishop Estate. I daresay that both Takabuki and Ching had something to do with the increase in annual profit from five percent of the Estate's 1970 valuation by nearly four hundred percent in the 1980s."

Richardson vehemently denied that he was ever a party to repayment of a Burns political debt to Takabuki.[35]

"I am my own man," he insisted, "and the Governor, of all persons, respected that."

In spite of the Chief Justice's denials and disavowals, the appearance of an injudicious mix of law and politics was at least as strong as the reality he claimed. In varying degrees and without a doubt, Richardson's opponents in the several controversial events of his early years on the bench represented valid points of view.

As Governor and Chief Justice, both Burns and Richardson were too politically skilled to be guilty of blatant collusion, Burns especially skilled in the language of direction through indirection. While neither may have influenced the other through the spoken word, their level of unspoken communication was deep enough, their shared goals compelling enough, that critics felt they were justified in sensing an unseemliness in the relationship between the executive and judicial branches of state government.

If one accepts the Chief Justice's claims, one also must see that at most, Richardson was guilty of a certain naivete in believing that reality was all that mattered. Even if one does not accept his remembered version of events, the Chief

Justice remains in good company: study of history reveals that the most esteemed of jurists often practiced both law and politics, unwittingly or not.

An intriguing factor in the three events described here—the Crossley-Mills suit, the Constitutional Convention discussion about the propriety of Burns' selection of Richardson as Chief Justice, the angry furor surrounding the High Court's selection of Takabuki as Bishop Estate trustee—was Richardson's pattern of behavior when under attack.

In these and other similar instances, the Chief Justice demonstrated a stoic and patient resistance, sometimes punctuated by retorts but more often by long silences. His silences were not marked by inactivity, for within the public silences he privately developed strategies for his defense, strategies which sometimes resulted in spokesmen who championed his position. During his silences, supporters came to his aid, opponents tripped themselves or fractionalized.

Part of his behavior stemmed from rational knowledge that judicial canons dictate a certain kind of temperance. Perhaps part of it also came out of a politician's instinct that timing is important if one intends to survive. And whether he "won" by instinct or rational design, by natural drift of events or imposition of his will, Richardson—under pressure—displayed traits which marked him as a survivor.

---

1. *Honolulu Star-Bulletin,* Byron Baker, Aug. 1, 1968. (Slight modification of quote for readibility.)

2. Until their duties took them out of Honolulu, Senator Daniel Inouye and Trust Territory High Commissioner William Norwood also were included in the group that met at the Kewalo Inn, later at Fort Street's Merchant Grill, then at Beaver Grill, and finally at Alakea Grill. The

operating rules were simple. The tab was picked up in alphabetical order, with the next person in line taking care of the tip. The person who paid usually brought a guest. At the death of a member the group invited someone to take his place; the invitation was extended only after informal, unanimous "election" to the group. The tradition continues to this day. The newest members, who were invited to join the group after the Governor's death in 1975 included James S. Burns, the Governor's son; Democrat leader Robert Oshiro; businessman Keiji Kawakami.

3. As it turned, the Supreme Court replacements—judges Albert Felix, Tom Okino, and Thomas Ogata—were indeed Burns appointees.

4. Insiders later claimed that the denial was not all that capricious. Crossley was his own worst enemy in seeking the governorship. Unable to accept the often necessarily oblique language of politics, he demanded that Eisenhower in no uncertain terms promise the governorship to him. This Eisenhower would not do prematurely. To have a demanding potential appointee at his heels annoyed him and marked Crossley as a political neophyte. Statement of Herman T. F. Lum in a conversation, Honolulu, Hawaii, Feb. 11, 1982. Others point out that Crossley had a powerful opponent in Hawaii's Delegate to Congress, Joseph P. Farrington, who vigorously pursued King's appointment. Statement of Masaji Marumoto, in a personal interview, Honolulu, Hawaii, Feb. 7, 1984.

5. Formation of the Foundation resulted from a 1967 conference organized by the Judiciary to encourage citizen participation in the administration of justice.

6. *Honolulu Star-Bulletin,* Harriet Gee, Dec. 26, 1978.

7. News articles of the day and more recent conversations with principal shapers of modern Hawaii produce an extraordinarily strong picture of Kobayashi. His character was marked by great discipline, perhaps the result of early training in judo (he was the youngest person in Hawaii to earn a Black Belt), a self-direction untainted by fear of public opinion; a practical plain-spokenness. The 1969 State Senate, breaking from tradition, affirmed his appointment to the High Court with a standing vote, which longtime political observers said was "a gesture of immense respect." *Honolulu Star-Bulletin, ibid.*

8. *Honolulu Advertiser,* July, 31, 1968.

9. *Ibid.*

10. *Proceedings of the Constitutional Convention of Hawaii of 1968,* Vol. II: Debates in Committee of the Whole (Honolulu: published under the supervision of the Administrator of the Convention, State of Hawaii, 1972), pp. 341–379.

11. Historically, Bishop Estate trustees had been *haoles* except for part-Hawaiians Edwin Murray, Samuel W. King and Richard Lyman.

12. *Wills and Deeds of Trust: Bernice P. Bishop Estate, Bernice P. Bishop Museum, Charles R. Bishop Trust* (Honolulu Hawaii: Printshop of Hawaii Co., Ltd. 3d Ed. 1957).

13. School charges have remained minimal because the Estate underwrites most of the Schools' operating costs and provides some tuition support to individuals based upon ability to pay.

14. To those who believed that Bishop Estate trustees easily could concentrate on both money-management and development of education for the Kamehameha Schools, trustee Hung Wo Ching made a disquieting statement in a speech before the Hawaiian Civic Club on Jan. 17, 1969: "It is unlikely that . . . trustees, individually or collectively, can efficiently administer both the business aspects of the Estate and the educational aspects of the Kamehameha Schools simultaneously." He went on to ask his audience: "If you were a trustee, which would you choose to do?" From office files of William S. Richardson.

15. Governor Burns' son, James, sees irony of sorts in the fact that his father's ties with the Japanese are so well chronicled when his strongest sympathies lay with the native Hawaiians. It is James Burns' contention that his father looked constantly for Hawaiians whom he could nurture. Most of them, according to the younger Burns, in time disappointed the Governor in one way or another. Thus, he claims, the Governor's continuing and growing pride in Richardson's accomplishments was a special kind of pride. Statement of James S. Burns, in a personal interview, Honolulu, Hawaii, April 26, 1982.

16. No known studies examine this antagonism. Aside from basic cultural differences, one explanation may be that as the Japanese ended their contracts with sugar plantations, they moved away from rural areas and into city jobs, displacing Hawaiians in the process.

17. The article was written by Brian Casey, a one-time *Honolulu Advertiser* newsman. Casey headed the City's Office of Information under Fasi's Republican predecessor Neal Blaisdell; served as elected Democrat City Councilman for one term; and was named Fasi's director of City Auditoriums upon losing his first bid for Council re-election. Casey's article also suggested that Blaisdell was "double-crossed" by Richardson and Burns when a Bishop Estate trustee's post—the *quid pro quo* for Blaisdell's refrainment from the gubernatorial campaign in 1966 and his retirement from the mayoralty in 1968—was given instead to Hung Wo Ching. "Honolulu News," Brian Casey, Jan. 29, 1971.

18. *Honolulu Advertiser,* June 28, 1971.
19. *Honolulu Advertiser,* June 25, 1971.
20. *Honolulu Star-Bulletin,* June 23, 1971.
21. Statement from the files of Masaji Marumoto. See also *Honolulu Advertiser,* June 30, 1971.
22. *Honolulu Star-Bulletin,* July 6, 1971.
23. In fact, King and Gill—joined by other lawyers including Arthur K. Trask—offered free legal services to the Ad Hoc Committee for a Hawaiian Trustee.
24. *Honolulu Advertiser,* June 23, 1971.
25. *Honolulu Star-Bulletin,* July 17, 1971.
26. *Honolulu Star-Bulletin,* June 22, 1971.
27. He would have stepped into the office earlier were it not for his request that he be allowed until July 30 to complete business transactions and sever conflict-of-interest ties.
28. *Honolulu Advertiser,* Feb. 12, 1972.
29. By "recusing" itself, the Supreme Court did not disqualify itself; it merely refused to sit as judge on that particular case.
30. Other attorneys on the team included Thomas M. Pico, Jr., and Edward Kemper. King subsequently was named federal judge, discontinued participation in the suit, and was replaced by Allan S. Haley.
31. *Honolulu Star Bulletin, April 4, 1973.*
32. Earlier, Richardson had indicated in testimony before the Constitutional Convention's Judicial Committee that if delegates wanted to involve more persons in the judicial selection process, he could accept the notion of a "judicial confirmation commission." This commission would screen judges selected by the governor. *Honolulu Star-Bulletin,* July, 11, 1978; *Honolulu Advertiser,* Douglas Woo, Aug. 25, 1978.
33. Statement of William S. Richardson in a personal interview, Honolulu, Hawaii, April 10, 1978.
34. Ching, in fact, sued Takabuki in a case which reached the State circuit court in February, 1982. The suit charged that Takabuki deliberately misled fellow trustees—who were less experienced in business and real estate—into purchase of property which was exorbitantly priced. Ching asserted that the developers, friends of Takabuki, would have sold the property for less. Ching continued to press his suit even after his friends advised him it was groundless, even after a federal court refused it on the grounds that federal issues were not involved. The circuit court ultimately found the trustees violated no fiduciary duties in completing the sale.

The Chief Justice professed no change of feelings toward either man, believing that each was motivated by a sincere desire to do his best for the Estate. However, an interesting mini-drama took place in the Friday lunch group, of which Ching was a member. James Burns, who had been invited to join the group after his father's death, expressed angry disappointment that Ching would take such public and divisive legal action; he refused to have lunch with "Mr. Ching" any more and tried to convince the others that they should follow his example. The others—Richardson, Ed Burns, McCabe, Oshiro, Inouye when he was in town—refused to let the temporary controversy divide a group generally unified in purpose for thirty years. Only businessman Keiji Kawakami, a relative newcomer to the group, felt discomfited enough to take leave from the lunches.

35. A 1982 conversation with retired Justice Masaji Marumoto gives credence to Richardson's insistence that he was not involved in repayment of a Burns debt to Takabuki. Marumoto's personal observation was that Burns habitually kept from encroaching upon judicial prerogatives. Furthermore, Marumoto revealed, when the appointment was met with great hostility by the Hawaiians, Richardson asked Marumoto privately whether it might not be a good idea for the High Court to nominate someone else "this time around."

"Although Takabuki was not my initial candidate for trustee," Marumoto said in 1982, "I backed him all the way when it became obvious *my* nominee did not have a chance. Three of us on the 1971 Court were Japanese [Abe and Kobayashi in addition to Marumoto]. If a Japanese *ever* were to be named Bishop Estate trustee, *then* was the time it could be done." Marumoto said he did not talk to either Abe or Kobayashi about racial ramifications of the pending Estate appointment. "The Chief Justice was the only one I talked to along these lines. He agreed with me that there was no reason a Japanese ought not to be named trustee." Statement of Masaji Marumoto, in a personal interview, Honolulu, Hawaii, May 28, 1982.

Photo Identification
Chapter II, p. 22
Governor John Anthony Burns with William S. Richardson in 1962 after their election as governor and lieutenant governor.

"I think it's fit to say: the true and sensitive Hawaiian, the sensitive Japanese, and the sensitive Chinese that I know, abhor this racial approach to decision in the law as much as I do."

J. Russell Cades, Attorney
February 20, 1980[1]

"This is a 'real people' court. These justices know the problems of the real world; they know how real people feel. They know especially how local people feel."

Wallace S. Fujiyama, Attorney
February 20, 1980[2]

III
Opinions of the Court

Although fabled as a melting pot of races, evidence of racial division resounds throughout island history. Individual and communal problems caused by clash of cultures surfaced and persisted in many forms over many years.

For example, Lot Kamehameha—King Kamehameha V—is said to have retreated into the Hawaiian past when the "civilized" rituals of his rule tired and confused him. Abandoning court dress and custom, he then would withdraw to his house at the seashore, eating, drinking, dancing, generally leading a life which was once the good life in ancient Hawaii, but which, under the set of Calvinist mores introduced by the white man, now bordered on debauchery.[3] It was as though he rewarded himself for proper Christian and Western behavior; at those times, he gave in to the other, more ancient culture tugging at his soul.

Later, public figures no less influential than King Kalakaua, the last male monarch of the kingdom, and Queen Liliuokalani, the sister who succeeded him, periodically objected to incursions of foreigners and of American missionaries on their culture.[4] Whatever their own foibles (and even

Liliuokalani could not decide whether her brother David was wastrel or saint), an enduring message they transmitted to their subjects was one of anger at being dispossessed, an anger which seemed alternately to strengthen their people and embitter them into ineffectiveness.

The tensions between native and non-native cultures grew more complex with influx of various immigrant groups to the islands during the latter half of the nineteenth century. These immigrant waves gave vitality to what might have become a vapid, insular society. They also affirmed old laws of societal behavior: newcomers are at the mercy of the established order until they gain enough economic and political power; and, the established order will do everything it can—legal or illegal—to keep the newest arrivals at the lowest point of the power structure.

In Hawaii, these laws underwent some permutation, giving subtle dimensions to the normal complexities of ethnic politics. For in few other places did immigrants of so many different races arrive in such a short span of time to make their home in such a small geographic area. Furthermore, they arrived to find erosion of the indigenous group's authority. They also found dominant overlay of American-European cultures upon Hawaiian life.

All of these factors resulted in a strange situation. Eventually, the island community became polarized into the all-powerful white elitists and the powerless non-white, numerically greater, indigenous and immigrant masses. Within each of the two groups were gradations of influence. The continuum between the two groups was sparsely populated by the ambivalent, usually Hawaiians who, at one moment, might cast their lot with *haole* rulers and, at another moment, might conclude that only by joining forces with other non-whites could they regain any real power.

Nowhere, perhaps, was the Hawaiian political ambivalence more visibly illustrated than in the family of Prince Kuhio and David Kawananakoa, sons of old island royalty. Kuhio, after spending a year in prison for taking part in the unsuccessful counterrevolution to restore Queen Liliuokalani to her throne, became a member of the Republican Party. His brother, David Kawananakoa, broke away from the native Home Rule Party in 1900 to organize the Democratic Party of Hawaii.[5] The family, though politically divided, remained united in its protests against the powerful strangers in their midst, in their attempts to regain some of what they and their people had lost.

Whatever their political affiliations, many native Hawaiians shared a desire to preserve their cultural identity and to keep the foreigners out. Coupled with unsophisticated campaign practices of an earlier time, this desire sometimes found serio-comic expression.

Consider the native politician in an early Territorial campaign who pointedly commented on the fact that his opponent was white. He stood at the polls on election day, shouting in Hawaiian at the top of his voice, "Look at the skin and [don't] vote for him."[6]

One of the earliest recorded protests against the threat of foreigners had occurred in 1845, when natives of Kailua on the Big Island presented a petition to their king, Kamehameha III, and their legislature. The natives, prescient in their concerns, had implored the chiefs not to sell lands to white men or other foreigners: "The selling of lands to outsiders is not a wise course, the lands being a source of benefit to the Government, the throne and the Hawaiian people."

Further, the natives had asked that foreigners be denied full citizenship in the kingdom and allowed to act in a governmental advisory post for only three to four years. Otherwise, the natives said, ". . . they will predominate over the chiefs, the throne, the Government, the people and the country, after . . . the chiefs are dead. Then the country will be taken away by the foreigners."[7]

The sweep of history would push this petition aside for more than a century.

Then the Richardson Court—delving into island history, apparently disregarding a century of established law in significant instances, attempting to rely upon and apply native concepts, practices and precedents—would reach across the years to address some of the concerns contained in the petition.

Even in his younger days, Bill Richardson's feelings about the islands' power structure were clearly defined. His intent to change that structure to a more equitable one became a persistent theme in his life, as did his intent somehow to reverse the flow of history and to better the lot of the Hawaiian. Like his father, he harbored no doubts that the Democratic Party was his Party. He mediated change through the Party from the early 1940s until 1966, working with others to strengthen the Party and, through the Party, to work toward Statehood and a community marked by equality for all its citizens.

When Richardson stepped on to the Supreme Court bench in 1966, the major personal and political themes of his life were clearly developed, awaiting only a more conducive court milieu—and the right cases—for further expression.

The retirement in May, 1967, of Justices Charles Cassidy and Rhoda Lewis, Republican appointees, and Cable Wirtz, a Democrat, ended what was viewed as an essentially moderate court. (A little ironically, Jack Mizuha, the last Republican appointee whose term would last until June of 1968, was considered a very progressive justice, even after addition of new justices of Democratic and ostensibly more liberal ideology.)

Just prior to the retirement of the three justices, a reporter assigned to the courts asked several attorneys to describe the legal-philosophic leanings of the departing jurists. Attorney Harriet Bouslog's reply was immediate: "Definitely conservative." Bouslog, a labor lawyer and the quintessence of flaming liberalism, could hardly be expected to reply otherwise. But in this instance, her judgment was confirmed by lawyers of disparate political persuasions.[8]

Always ready to expound her precise meaning, Bouslog said that a "conservative" court was one reluctant to depart from legal precedent, one which—in her opinion—tended too often to take too legalistic a view of the law.[9]

In just a short while, Bouslog would have little reason to describe Hawaii's High Court as "too legalistic." In a short while, even some judicial activists—those who, in varying degrees, felt it the bench's prerogative to venture into the role of public policy-maker—would express uneasiness at the Court's extremely activist approach to law. Many observers also were discomfited by what seemed to be a racial approach to legal decision-making. This approach, if not racial, at least appeared to be biased toward "local" peoples as opposed to "outsiders" or newcomers to the islands.

In May of 1967, Masaji Marumoto, Kazuhisa Abe, and Bernard H. Levinson stepped into vacancies created by the retiring Republican justices. Marumoto and Levinson balanced each other in an interesting way. Both graduates of Harvard Law School, they appeared to share a careful, scholarly, ratiocinative approach to law. Marumoto was the only Republican appointed by Governor Burns to the Supreme Court.[10] Levinson was a Democrat whose affections lay with groups such as the American Civil Liberties Union. Although Marumoto and Levinson often disagreed vehemently with each other in the privacy of the Supreme Court conference room, they sometimes found themselves together as fellow dissenters to the Supreme Court majority.[11]

Kazuhisa Abe filled the last High Court vacancy in 1967.

Like Marumoto, he had been raised in a rural community on the Big Island. But he was a Democrat and had served for many years in the State Senate, the last few of them as Senate president. Like Levinson, he held liberal views; unlike Levinson, however, his public expression of these views often was explosive. Outspoken, he sometimes bordered on an inarticulateness bred partly of impatience, partly of very strong feelings, and partly of an early background where pidgin English was the normal mode of communication.

In July, 1969, Bert Kobayashi, Sr., Governor Burns' first Attorney General and a man with a reputation as a tough, forthright negotiator, was named to fill the vacancy created by Justice Mizuha's retirement in June, 1968.

The State Supreme Court, for the first time, now consisted entirely of members appointed by John Burns. The Governor, as he appointed them, reportedly told some of them not to feel bound by Territorial precedents if, in their judgment, those precedents were wrong. Territorial judges and governors named by U.S. presidents usually had no roots in Hawaii, and Burns and his Party perceived them as largely unfamiliar with and unsympathetic to special island conditions.[12]

To suggest that the prior body of Anglo-American law is not sacrosanct comes close to heresy in some legal circles; to act upon that suggestion is even more damnable.

Through a series of decisions stretching from the late 1960s through the next decade, Hawaii's Supreme Court would show a willingness to defy the existing body of Anglo-American case law. In rendering its decisions in these cases, the Court recognized the validity of both native Hawaiian and Anglo-American tenets of jurisprudence. At points of unresolvable conflict and contradiction between the two cultures, the Court often would leap backward in time to draw upon precepts and traditions of the Hawaiian culture.[13]

Harsh critics of these decisions charged the Richardson Court with tyranny and heresy. The Court, they said, assumed lawmaking and public policy-making authority which was assigned to other government bodies. Other critics of these Court decisions raised their concerns in gentler fashion.

A *Star-Bulletin* editorial, for example, acknowledged that many people understood and sympathized with the underlying reasons for these decisions. But, the editorial continued:

> The danger in such a course . . . is that the whole foundation of law in the state, as developed and interpreted through most of this century, can now be said to be undermined and uncertain. No man can be sure that a contract means much in these circumstances.[14]

In a decision issued in mid-1968, *Palama* v. *Sheehan,* Richardson gave the first indication that he considered ancient Hawaiian practices valid precedent for modern legal decisions. Demonstrating his rich knowledge of the island past, the Chief Justice wrote a unanimous decision upholding a Kauai circuit court decision which based modern rights upon the ancient rights to use of the land.[15] The decision retains some historical interest because it illustrates for the very first time the Richardson Court's willingness to transpose a customary Hawaiian right to a present-day context.

The customary Hawaiian right of land usage which had been developed over several centuries underwent some adjustment and codification after Kamehameha III's 1848 Great Mahele, which distributed land among the king, the *alii* chiefs, and commoners. The Mahele, which ended the semi-feudal ownership of land, was followed by the Kuleana Act of 1850.[16] The Act allowed native Hawaiians to apply to the Kingdom's Land Commission for a *kuleana,* a small parcel of land awarded in fee. Certain rights accrued to the owner of a *kuleana,* which sometimes fell within an *ahupuaa,* a larger plot of land stretching from sea to mountain.

In a modern case which had its roots in Hawaiian land usage, the Philip K. Palamas filed a suit to get clear title to a large tract of land known as Nomilo Pond in Kalaheo, on the island of Kauai. The Palamas' land covered some sixty acres and included an eighteen-acre fishing pond. John J. Sheehan, along with a few other persons, owned four *kuleana*s. Three of their *kuleana*s fell directly outside the seaward boundary of the Palama property, one fell within the boundary. In filing an answer to the Palama suit, Sheehan asserted his claim to fishing rights in the pond and right-of-way through the Palama property. He based his claim upon ancient Hawaiian rights.

Kauai's circuit court ruled that Sheehan did *not* have the right to fish in the pond but was entitled to reasonable right-of-way privileges through the Palamas' land for exit and entry to his own property.

On appeal, the Palamas argued that Sheehan had not proved existence of an ancient right-of-way through the acreage in dispute. Furthermore, they contended, the judge had not specified "right-of-way" in definite enough terms: if he granted right-of-way on the basis of old Hawaiian practice, then he should not permit use of modern motor vehicles through the Palama land, and the entry and exit path should be wide enough only for persons on foot or on horseback.

The Palamas' argument was one which was not brooked by the Chief Justice.

Upholding the decision of the lower court, Richardson pointed out that in old Hawaii, whenever a *kuleana* fell within boundaries of an *ahupuaa,* the rights of the native owner of the *kuleana* were specifically reserved, *"Koe no kuleana o Kanaka."* To support his statement, Richardson cited *kuleana* land owner rights which were included in the August 6, 1850, Act of the Hawaiian Kingdom.

The Palama decision, based upon old Hawaiian laws and practices, preserved the integrity of native customs and history without undermining the bulwark of later Western laws; it thus was accepted by the public with little comment.[17] The decision did not hint at future similarly-based decisions of the Richardson Court which would lead to bursts of indignation in some segments of the island community.

These later decisions would deal with issues involving ownership of land and water. The Richardson Court consistently would favor State and public ownership of property over ownership by private interests. These decisions would be met with great consternation by legal conservatives and traditionalists, who viewed them as shocking, almost capricious, disjunctions of the law.

Two of Hawaii's precious resources, fresh water and the shoreline, served as focal points for the Richardson Court's judicial activism. Before statehood, these resources were considered to be private commodities, subject to the exclusive use and control of landowners who either owned property upon which they were located or property adjacent to them. (Students of island history, particularly those with a revisionist bent, are fond of pointing out that pre-statehood notions of ownership favored planters and that small band of men who were arbiters of the sugar-based island economy.)

Water and shoreline decisions of the Richardson Court upset earlier notions of ownership. In making its decisions, the Court relied heavily upon three factors: its view of King Kamehameha III's intent at the time of the Mahele; known ancient Hawaiian customs and practices; and *kamaaina* testimony with regard to those customs and practices.[18]

Underlying each of the controversial water and beach decisions was a single theme—that, in translating the indigenous system into a Western system, inadequate consideration had been given to the long-held rights of a native people who had relied upon their king to protect their interests and well-being.

The vehicle for the Court's reassertion of the public's claim to water would come to be known as the McBryde case. It began quietly in 1959 as a dispute between two adjacent sugar plantations in the Hanapepe Valley on the island of Kauai. In that year the McBryde Sugar Company brought suit against its neighbor, Gay and Robinson, to determine their relative rights to waters of the Hanapepe River and the Koula and Manuahi Streams which fed it. Other parties to the suit subsequently included the State of Hawaii, Olokele Plantation and small landowners in the Hanapepe valley.

Three different types of water rights were asserted. The first of these rights were "appurtenant," attached to lands on the basis of the amount of water used at the time those lands were converted into private ownership. The second were "prescriptive," gained through actual use of given amounts of water against the rights of others during a statutorially required period of time. The third were rights to "surplus" water, the rest of the river waters. Earlier judicial decisions had established water as a private commodity that could be used without restriction, subject to no higher authority than the private rights of its owners.

Presentation of the various claims in the lower court consumed a decade. Finally, in a 1969 decision, the Kauai court quantified the appurtenant rights of each party, awarded McBryde certain prescriptive rights, and granted surplus water rights to Robinson as the owner, or *konohiki,* of the property upon which the Hanapepe river waters originated.[19] Robinson, McBryde and the State then appealed to the Supreme Court on various grounds.

In December of 1973, Hawaii's Supreme Court partially overturned the judgment of the Kauai circuit court and announced a dramatically new doctrine of water rights. Largely ignoring Hawaiian case law since the turn of the century, the Richardson Court went back to the time of the monarchy in an attempt to determine the intent of native kings with respect to water rights. The Court came to a clear conclusion: grants of water rights to landowners by kings had been limited to actual need, and other water had been reserved for public use. The Court then declared that Hawaii's waters no longer were a privately owned commodity: although recognizing private appurtenant rights, it reserved the basic ownership of all waters to the State, prohibited the transfer of appurtenant rights, and abolished the concepts of prescriptive rights and of surplus water.[20]

Justice Abe wrote the majority decision, relying heavily upon interpretation of 1846 and 1850 laws of the kingdom. Justice Marumoto was sole dissenter. (Marumoto later was joined by Justice Levinson after a rehearing.) The assertion of the majority opinion was clear: in treating water as a private commodity, public interests had been sacrificed for the benefit of a handful of large property owners. The Richardson Court, in its McBryde decision, sought to redress this situation by denying commercial ownership of water and recognizing the State as ultimate arbiter for distribution of water.

The ruling was totally unexpected by the attorneys for the major plantations involved in the suit. They, and others with a traditional view of the law, were incensed.

They protested that the Court's decision centered on an issue which was not even in dispute. Parties to the original suit, they said, *never* believed that public ownership of water was at issue; rather, the concern of the plantations was further definition and quantification of their respective rights to and ownership of water.

Some attorneys expressed the feeling that the Richardson Court always had intended, one way or another, to deal with the issue of public rights to and ownership of water whether or not that issue actually came before the Court.[21]

The most severe critics of the Hanapepe decision asked a hard question: Since when did a state supreme court have the right to take what was deemed private property by legal precedent and to give that property away to the State?

A rehearing was scheduled in the State Supreme Court, but the decision remained the same.

An appeal to the U.S. Supreme Court was turned down.

Undaunted, and united in their belief that the Richardson Court wrongfully had usurped property, McBryde joined with Robinson, Olokele, and Hanapepe Valley farmers to challenge the decision in the U.S. District Court.

The basis of their challenge was the allegation that taking private property without just compensation was a constitutional violation and hence subject to federal court jurisdiction.

In 1977, District Court judge Martin Pence issued an injunction against the enforcement of the Richardson Court's decision, in effect reversing it. Pence minced no words: the State Supreme Court had erred in its radical departure from prior decisions and in its usurpation of property without fair payment.[22] Discussing the case even years after his decision, Pence's comments were strong and direct, typifying not only a personal characteristic but also the high feelings which continue to stamp discussion about the Hanapepe case.

The High Court's ruling was "strictly a 'public policy' decision with no prior underlying 'legal' justification," Pence said. "It was ". . . one of the grossest examples of unfettered judicial construction used to achieve the result desired—regardless of its effect upon the parties, or the state of the prior law on the subject."[23]

In more temperate language, Justices Marumoto and

Levinson had made much the same points in their dissenting opinions, Marumoto additionally pointing out the decision's negative impact upon those for whom irrigation systems formed an economic backbone.[24]

The State of Hawaii took Pence's "reversal" to the U.S. Ninth Circuit Court of Appeals. In May, 1981, the Ninth Circuit asked the State High Court to answer six "certified questions" in order to clarify the meaning and effect of the Court's 1973 decision and its relationship to prior Hawaii decisions. In December, 1982, after briefing and oral argument by all parties, the Court issued answers to the questions in a lengthy opinion authored by Richardson.[25] In August, 1983, following Richardson's retirement from the bench, the remaining members of the Court denied a motion to reconsider the opinion, and the answers then formally transmitted to the Ninth Circuit.

Throughout reactive developments stemming from the Supreme Court's reversal of the 1959 decision of the Kauai court, Richardson remained quietly confident. He refused to disqualify himself from the case. He was certain that his Court's *McBryde* decision was justified. In private conversations with his friends, Richardson expressed feelings of hurt and disappointment at Pence's injunction and statements to the press. It seemed to the Chief Justice that Pence's written and spoken language was injudicious and inappropriate, aimed personally at Richardson himself rather than at the issues in the case.

The Chief Justice had reached his position only after extensive research and lengthy discussions with other justices, particularly with Marumoto; for a long time, he had not been certain at all what his decision would be. Once his decision was made, however, he was confident that it was correct. Richardson's confidence extended to decisions in the area of land ownership as well.

Over the period of a decade, several cases confirmed his Court's intent to base some of its decisions upon Hawaiian, rather than Anglo-American, law and practice. Hawaii's Supreme Court extended the same Hanapepe principle of public ownership, this time to beachfront land, through decisions in the 1968 *Ashford* case, the 1973 *Sotomura* case, the 1977 *Sanborn* case, and the 1977 *Zimring* case.[26]

The *Ashford* case, the first of what would be called the Shoreline Boundary Cases, involved property on the island of Molokai.[27] The High Court's *Ashford* decision was important in that it revealed the basic approach and philosophy of the Richardson Court toward ownership of beachfront property. The decision also revealed how much credence the Court would place upon the testimony of *kama'aina* witnesses, persons whose knowledge of and connection with the land were so deep that they could attest expertly to pre-1892 native custom.

The Clinton Ashfords had petitioned the land court in 1963 to register title to property granted by royal patents in 1866. The original patents described the seaward boundary as *ma ke kai,* translated to "along the sea." The U.S. Coast and Geodetic Survey provided tidal information supporting the Ashfords' contention that this boundary lay at the mean high water line.

The land court ruled in favor of the Ashfords.

The State of Hawaii contested the land court decision, basing its case on what it termed "reputation evidence" presented by "*kama'aina* witnesses." The State claimed that the term *ma ke kai* did not refer to the mean high water mark; it referred instead to the high water mark at the debris or vegetation line.

The justices, particularly Richardson and Marumoto, engaged in lengthy, earnest conversations about the pending decision, which Richardson felt was a most important one.[28]

The crux of the matter, as far as Richardson was concerned, lay in the king's intent when he gifted others with shoreline property. Richardson felt that no Hawaiian king would deny his subjects access to beach frontage for any number of public uses: for sorting *limu,* or seaweed; for beaching canoes; for swimming and other recreational activities.

Marumoto agreed that the king's intent was important, but more important was the fact that native rulers, in time, had accepted Western standards and influence. One of the consequences of such acceptance, Marumoto firmly believed, was strict adherence to Western scientific measurements and Western legal concepts as developed through case and common law.

After serious deliberation among the justices, the Chief Justice wrote the majority opinion. He upheld the State's position and rejected years of common law in declaring that the upper reaches of the waves, usually indicated by the debris or vegetation line, formed the new shoreline boundary between private and public lands.[29]

Richardson asserted that King Kamehameha V certainly had no knowledge of standards applied by the U.S. Coast and Geodetic Survey, formally established in the islands only in 1929. Thus, interpretation of the King's intent must depend upon "reputation evidence," and this evidence must prevail over any evidence produced by standards of a later time.[30]

Justice Marumoto again found himself the dissenter, as he would in other Shoreline Boundary cases. This time he felt so strongly that his written opinion extended for forty-two pages.[31] Usually polite and circumspect even in disagreement, this time Marumoto's language of dissent revealed the passion of his feelings.

In his written opinion, Marumoto claimed that the State's position was based on "spurious historical assumptions" and that there was no reason "for Hawaii to deviate from the mainstream of American decisions." The Supreme Court's decision, he said, was a practice which the U.S. Supreme Court had rejected for use by the Federal Government; the State Court's decision encouraged "a practice primitive in concept and haphazard in application and result."[32]

The majority opinion in *Ashford* soon was followed by similar opinions. The *Sotomura* and *Sanborn* Supreme Court decisions consistently affirmed the *Ashford* principle of shoreline ownership although the basic facts in each case differed.

Joseph Y. Sotomura owned land in the Black Sand area of the Big Island. Hawaii County, which wanted to improve its beach park, claimed that the shoreline portion of one of Sotomura's lots was public land. Sotomura disagreed, producing land title registration which showed that the original boundary had been washed away by erosion and was now under water. He asserted that the shoreline portion of his property was *not* public property.

The circuit judge ruled that because of the erosion which had occurred, the court had to draw a new boundary line. Since the property line enunciated in the earlier *Ashford* decision was the debris or vegetation line, the court simply drew a new line at the vegetation line.

Sotomura appealed his case to the Hawaii Supreme Court, only to have it uphold the circuit court's decision. The High Court made no bones about its assumption of a policy-making role: "Public policy as interpreted by this court, favors extending to public use and ownership as much of Hawaii's shoreline as is reasonably possible."[33]

The Supreme Court made a number of important statements through its *Sotomura* decision. First, it said that while erosion may alter the size of oceanfront property, it does not alter the placement of the seaward boundary according to the standard set forth by *Ashford*. Secondly, it declared that when high tides are evidenced both by a debris line and a vegetation line, the vegetation line is presumptively the property's shoreline boundary.

The *Sotomura* case was the subject of a separate action in federal district court.[34] The Sotomuras alleged that the Hawaii Supreme Court's determination of a new seaward boundary constituted a taking of private property in violation of the U.S. Constitution. The federal district court agreed and enjoined enforcement of the decision. Misunderstanding and bureaucratic bungling prevented the State of Hawaii from filing a timely notice of appeal; it therefore could not carry out its intent to take the case to the Ninth Circuit Court of Appeals.

However, the Supreme Court was able to reassert its position a few years after the original *Sotomura* decision through its decision in the *Sanborn* case. Like the Sotomuras, heirs to the estate of Walter F. Sanborn held a land court decree which placed a boundary of their property seaward of the vegetation line. The Sanborn heirs, joint owners of Hanalei Bay property on Kauai, wished to subdivide their lot; application of the Supreme Court's *Ashford* principle would reduce the size of their lot to the point where they could not subdivide it under Kauai ordinances.

Legal traditionalists pessimistically pointed out that if the Sanborn heirs thought that their 1951 land court title provided sufficient legal proof of acreage perimeters, they were mistaken. After all, they were dealing with a Supreme Court which, in the *Ashford* case, had interpreted a royal patent with self-assurance and had ignored long-practiced U.S. Coast and Geodetic principles. It was a Court which had ridden out accusations of "uninhibited judicial lawmaking" by articulate and powerful critics, among them J. Russell Cades, the attorney for McBryde in the Hanapepe water rights case and a partner in an old, large, and prestigious law firm.[35] It was a Court which, in the *Sotomura* case, calmly had established a new boundary line in the face of shoreline erosion. Expectably, the State Supreme Court ruled that the land court had erred in its *Sanborn* decree.

The 1977 *Zimring* case provided a foil against which the ramifications of Hawaii's shoreline boundary cases could be examined further.

The Puna lava flow of 1955 had changed the boundaries of Big Island property owned by Herbert C. Shipman, destroying the existing oceanfront boundary and adding 7.9 acres of lava in the process. Five years later, the Maurice Zimrings bought and proceeded to improve the entire property, including the newly-formed lava addition. In 1968, in its attempt to claim that portion of the property formed by the lava flow, the State filed a suit against the Zimrings in circuit court.

In some ways, the case incorporated key elements of two of the Shoreline Boundary Cases. In *Sotomura,* private property had been decreased by erosion; in the *Zimring* case, it had been increased by lava deposit. In *Ashford,* the State had presented testimony from two *kama'aina* witnesses; in the *Zimring* case, the defendants—perhaps noting the High Court's deference to such testimony—produced a witness to testify on their behalf. Land surveyor William Kamau, born in 1892 and professing to have expert knowledge of ancient Hawaiian land practices, testified that new land formed by lava flows belonged to the abutting land owner.

The circuit judge ruled in favor of the Zimrings, basing his decisions upon the historical evidence presented by Kamau and also upon the "matter of basic and fundamental fairness" to the Zimrings.[36]

The State's appeal to the Supreme Court resulted in reversal of the lower court's ruling.

1. Newly-commissioned Chief Justice William Richardson (r.), with Hawaii's Governor John Burns at his side, walks from Iolani Palace to Ali'iolani Hale's Supreme Court courtroom to take his oath of office on March 25, 1966.

2. A very young William Shaw Richardson, some forty years away from Hawaii's chief justiceship, is flanked by his sisters Grace (l.) and Amy (r.) as he rings in a new year.

3. The family of Wilfred and Amy Richardson pose for a family portrait in the 1930s: (seated, from l.) Pearl, mother Amy Lan Kyau Wung, father Wilfred Kelelani Kanekoa Alapai, Grace; (standing, from l.) Robert, Arlon, William, and Amy.

4. After graduation from Roosevelt High School, Richardson earned his B.A. in business and economics from the University of Hawaii (UH) in 1941, later receiving a J.D. degree in 1943 and an honorary LL.D. in 1967 from the University of Cincinnati's Law School. In his senior year at the UH, Richardson was one of eleven students selected by classmates to receive an honorary Real Dean medal.

5. Richardson swam on the UH's team for four years, serving as captain in his senior year. Here he is shown with teammates who took the island championship, 400 meter relay: (from l.) Charles Miyata, Vernon Dang, Richardson, Gerald Greenwell.

6. During World War II from 1943 to 1946, Richardson began his legal career as assistant staff judge advocate general, U.S. Army, Pacific. For a while, he was stationed in Leyte, serving with the First Filipino Infantry Regiment.

7. An informal photo shows young parents Bill and Amy Richardson with their children: (from l.) Corinne Kahaulani ("Reenie"), William Kahelelani (Billy), and Barbara Piimaile ("Bebe").

8. Richardson and Amy Corinne Ching were married June 21, 1947 at St. Andrew's Cathedral by longtime friend and Episcopal bishop of Honolulu Harry S. Kennedy. Members of the wedding party included: (from l.) Robert Richardson, Raymond Won Pat O'Sullivan, bridegroom Bill, bride Amy, Barbara Ching, Linnie Young, Pearl Richardson, Arlon Richardson, and Albert Tanji.

9. The Richardson family established strong ties with the Episcopal Church, Bill Richardson serving as warden of the Church of the Epiphany in Kaimuki for many years. Here Richardson poses with The Rev. Burton L. Linscott (l.), pastor at Epiphany and The Right Rev. Harry S. Kennedy (r.), bishop of Honolulu from 1944 to 1969.

10. Richardson was active in the Democratic Party until his appointment as Chief Justice in 1966. Here he is shown with Republican Hiram Fong, U.S. Representative and later Senator from Hawaii; both men were part of an island contingent of public officials which flew to Washington, D.C., in the early 1950s to present the case for Hawaiian Statehood.

11. Gus Sproat (l.) and his wife Abbie shake hands with the Chief Justice at Richardson's retirement party in December, 1982. Sproat, Supreme Court bailiff from 1926 and Chief Clerk from 1944 to 1966, participated in the Chief Justice's 1966 swearing-in ceremony.

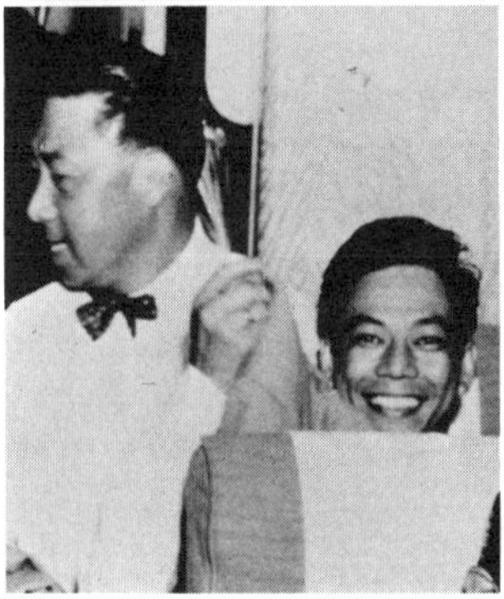

Chief Justice Richardson, in writing the majority decision, refuted Kamau's testimony by pointing to the scarcity of lava flows which altered privately owned oceanfront land, only two between 1846 and 1892. Custom could hardly result from such a limited occurrence of eruptions, he implied.

Richardson restated a major pre-Mahele principle, one adopted by his Court in most of its majority decisions on land and water cases: *ahupuaa*s, intended to be self sufficient land divisions, really were held in trust for all people by the landowner *konohiki,* with all lands ultimately being held in trust by the king as overall *konohiki.* This remained so no matter how land was distributed. Extending this principle to the present time, the modern *konohiki,* the State, became trustee of land and water for all island peoples.

Furthermore, Richardson did not view the lava addition as common law "accretion," although the press and public continued to use that term in its discussion of the case.

In the years after the decision, Richardson staunchly would defend the *Zimring* decision, saying that, of course, it defied the law developed over the years in accretion cases. For, he insisted, land changes due to volcanic eruption were *not* caused by "accretion," the slow build-up of land deposit; they were caused by common law "avulsion," the sudden cataclysmic changes brought about by floods, avalanches, and similar natural events.

The *Sanborn* and *Zimring* decisions had been rendered by a Supreme Court whose composition was changed a little by the addition of new justices. In early 1974, Thomas S. Ogata and Benjamin Menor, both former State senators and then circuit judges, filled vacancies created by the retirement of Justices Marumoto and Abe. While neither had been part of the inner, original core of the earliest Democratic fighters, their backgrounds were akin to many other Burns appointees: their outlook was shaped by their immigrant heritage and their primary identification with non-Western cultures; also, their climb to success was achieved first, through education and then, through politics.[37] In mid-1975, Baird H. Kidwell filled the vacancy created by Justice Levinson's retirement. Kidwell was Republican, Stanford Law School-educated, impeccably credentialed in every respect. However, as a conservative and as a mainlander who had married into a *haole, kama'aina* family, his communication with other court members did not flow easily, instinctively, from the same wellspring of experience. Although the *Sanborn* case was heard after his appointment to the bench, he excused himself from the case.[38]

Besides the controversial land and water decisions which emanated from the Richardson Court, other decisions illustrated the Court's liberal bent. Some of these reinterpreted the statute of limitation in a much broader way. For instance, in one case, the High Court said that the medical malpractice statute did not begin to run until the victim was aware of her difficulty.[39] State Supreme Court decisions also tended to be protective of defendants' rights, continuing the national trends of the 1960s which expanded the rights of persons accused of a crime.[40] The right of citizens to bring suit also was broadened: a High Court decision that taxpayers could challenge the propriety of a legislative appropriation; another decision established the right of citizens to challenge land use decisions.[41]

As the controversy continued, especially after the land and water decisions, Bill Richardson would say, with a smile, in private conversations: "If I had my way, the public would have even greater access to water and shoreline property. Hawaiian kings, I'm sure, intended to give their subjects more public seashore lands than we now allot. No one but a fool would leave his canoe at the vegetation line and let the waves wash it out to sea! The kings *really* must have intended to extend public property to that area on the beach where canoes could be left without danger of being washed away."

With a broader smile, Richardson would then say: "But there's no point in drawing *blood* from my critics!"

Not a born orator, the Chief Justice was never more eloquent than when speaking to Hawaiians about their future based upon their past.

Early in 1974, Richardson had spoken at a large gathering of the Hawaiian Civic Clubs. His speech was surprisingly frank for one whose usual public demeanor was marked by restraint.

Richardson talked about the foreign system of laws and government which had been imposed upon "our own people." "*Haole* law," he said, had made crimes of what the Hawaiians considered "proper or trivial." "*Haole* law" had caused land to be taken away "illegally" from natives. Richardson went on to say that it was time for Hawaiians to work within the system to change the ills of the past.[42]

Richardson's central meaning was that modern day Hawaiians must and could work within the *haole* system to alter their condition.

Nearly everyone in his audience understood this meaning. Outside his immediate audience, in the wider community, there were those who felt an uneasiness at the latent militancy and potential divisiveness inherent in his words. A few worried persons knew the power of words to shape reality, and they feared the possible effects of Richardson's speech on some of his listeners.

Some students of history view events as discrete, unconnected occurrences often perverse in their defiance of cause and effect. Others believe, in spite of life's occasional absurdities, that history is marked generally by logical, causative progression from one event to another. Those who fall into this second category could claim that the decisions on water rights, access to and ownership of lands, were predetermined by island history and by the individual histories of the men who sat on the Richardson Court.

To be sure, such a claim begs many questions. What is the proper exercise of judicial authority? Where is the golden mean between judicial activism and adherence to the prior body of law? How far can the courts go in substituting the personal will of judges for the impersonal will of legal precedent? A further, tantalizing question is this: Exactly how "impersonal" is the will of legal precedent?

In handing down its controversial decisions on land and water rights, the Richardson Court seemed to use as its test the same test used by the U.S. Supreme Court led by Earl Warren.[43] In deciding these cases, Hawaii's jurists did not ask primarily, "What is the legal precedent? What is the law?" They asked instead, "What is fair?"

"Fair," like many other human qualities depends upon several variables for its definition. One variable—voiced by Wally Fujiyama, loud champion of the "local" as opposed to the "outsiders' " point of view—is this: "It depends whose ox is being gored."[44]

In the eyes of the island justices who supported the majority position in these cases, it *was* "fair" to give access to land and water to the public. Their opinions were justified, they may have felt, by an island history which often had denied the common man much of what once was his to use.

In private, Richardson's description of the Great Mahele was much more candid than his public utterances: the white man had sold Kamehameha III a "bill of goods" through the Mahele. Some of Richardson's belief contained seeds of romanticism, an appealingly skewed vision of the noble savage. He was convinced that *haole* civilization had deprived the native Hawaiian of much of his own civilization.

Surely, an entire culture could not be restored to a people through judicial fiat, but Richardson believed that if no one else would do it, it was his judicial duty to at least return some island property to its "rightful" owners.

One might say that through these decisions, the Richardson Court merely attempted to correct imbalances created by island history and by earlier island courts, courts which appeared to have a bias toward the ruling hegemony and commercial interests with a great deal at stake in protecting private rather than public ownership of land and water resources.

Whatever the final decisions from the federal courts, there will be no final answers. For, ultimately, questions about the "proper" exercise of judicial authority turn into a statement, a recognition of a human condition described by Oliver Wendell Holmes: "The life of the law has not been logic; it has been experience. The felt necessities of the time, the prevalent moral and political theories, intuitions of public policy, avowed or unconscious . . . have had a good deal more to do than the syllogism in determining the rules by which men should be governed."[45]

The controversial decisions of the Richardson Court seem to support Holmes' inference that even lawyers and judges, those most prudent and rational of creatures, do not escape the pull of passions, intuitions, and what they perceive to be the "felt necessities of the time."

Since the unspoken rule of confidentiality covers conference room discussions held by members of the State Supreme Court, Richardson's real role in the formulation of his court's controversial decisions will remain unknown. His general comments about the decisions indicate that he did not take a leadership role in the early stages of deliberation. His uncertainties, as well as his personal habit, led him instead to question, listen, research and converse with his Supreme Court brethren about the issues in each case. He spent especially long hours talking with dissenter Marumoto: "If anyone with as fine a legal mind as Maru believed as strongly as he did in *his* position, then it behooved me to be very sure that I had grounds for my position."[46] Once the Court's decisions were made, however, Richardson as Chief Justice and member of the court majority became spokesman and unwavering defender of these decisions.

Thus, while the Chief Justice's specific role in the decision-making process cannot be known, what is clear is that decisions issued by his court during his sixteen-year tenure changed the complexion of island justice.

Like courts throughout the nation, Hawaii's judiciary began to follow liberal trends of the 1960s which expanded rights of the accused and which generally broadened access of citizens to their courts.

More importantly, although considered "legally" unjustifiable by conservatives, the controversial decisions of the Richardson-led court altered Hawaii law that it became more reflective of the islands' uncommon cultural heritage.

---

1. *Honolulu Advertiser,* Gerald Kato and Ken Kobayashi, Feb. 20, 1980. (Slight modification of quote for readability.)

2. *Ibid.*

3. Isabella L. Bird, *Six Months in the Sandwich Islands* (Honolulu: University of Hawaii Press for Friends of the Library of Hawaii, 1964), p. 274.

4. Strong antagonisms based upon race and ethnicity existed long before the time of these last monarchs. Numerous instances of anti-*haole* feelings are recorded: the uprising on Maui (see Privy Council Minutes, July 14 and August 15, 1848, Vol. 4, 425–426, 430–446, Archives of Hawaii); the anti-American feelings held by earlier monarchs Alexander Liholiho and his brother Lot Kamehameha (see Jacob Adler, ed., *The Journal of Prince Alexander Liholiho: The Voyages Made to the United States, England and*

France in 1849–1850 (Hawaii: The University of Hawaii Press for the Hawaiian Historical Society, 1967); the crystallization of anti-foreign and anti-American sentiment during the 1874 elections, feelings which led to the rallying cry, "Hawaii for Hawaiians."

5. In 1900, David Kawananakoa was Democratic candidate for the post of delgate to Congress, running unsuccessfully against Republican Col. Samuel Parker and the ultimately victorious Home Rule candidate, Robert Wilcox. Two years later, Prince Kuhio would win election as the islands' Republican delegate to Congress and remain in that post until his death twenty years later.

6. In the short run of events, the native politician was not all that ineffective, for he won that particular election. Robert C. M. Littler, *The Governance of Hawaii* (California: Stanford University Press, 1929), p. 90.

7. Kailua, June 12, 1845, petition to Kamehameha III and the legislature, F.O. & Ex., 1845, Archives of Hawaii.

8. *Honolulu Star-Bulletin,* May 5, 1967.

9. *Ibid.*

10. Marumoto's lifelong allegiance to the Republican Party was unusual for someone of his age, race and rural background. (His father, a Japanese immigrant, first worked for the Paauhau sugar plantation; later, after a short trip back to Japan, he operated a general merchandise store in Honolulu, then in Kona.) His Republicanism came from an indebtedness he felt toward key Party members as he started his legal career: Governor Samuel W. King, Delegate Joseph P. Farrington and Farrington's wife Betty (who became Hawaii's Delegate to Congress after her husband's death.) In spite of his Republican loyalties, Marumoto maintained a closeness to Democratic leader Burns, a closeness built upon mutual esteem which grew over the years; they had met initially through their work with island Japanese during the war years. Statement by Masaji Marumoto, in a personal interview, Honolulu, Hawaii, May 21, 1982.

11. Levinson was chagrined whenever he, who prided himself on being a liberal, was linked with Marumoto, a recognized conservative. Once, when an *Advertiser* article described the Supreme Court as generally liberal with a "tinge of conservatism in the views of Justices Marumoto and Levinson in special types of cases," Levinson was very upset. *Honolulu Advertiser,* June 7, 1968; statement by Masaji Marumoto, in a personal interview, Honolulu, Hawaii, May 21, 1982.

12. Statement by James S. Burns, the Governor's son, in personal interviews, Honolulu, Hawaii, May 26, 1982 and Feb. 14, 1984.

13. The very first section of the Hawaii Revised Statutes, Section 1-1, provided some of the legal support for the Court's unusual deviations from Anglo-American law. The statute declared common law for the islands to be English common law as interpreted and defined through English and American decisions. However, the statute continued, exceptions could occur when that common law differed from Hawaiian use and Hawaiian judicial precedent. This statute in part provided basis for the Court's controversial decisions, giving it authority—some said license—for its actions.

14. *Honolulu Star Bulletin,* Feb. 14, 1974.

15. *Palama* v. *Sheehan,* 50 Hawaii 298, 440 P.2d 95 (1968).

16. 2 Rev. Law of Hawaii 2141 (1925).

17. In confirming the lower court's decision, the High Court relied in part upon a traditional doctrine of easement by necessity, a fundamental Western rule of property which in this case buttressed the native Hawaiian right.

18. Research had shown that in the islands long ago, certain people had been taught the names of boundaries of land divisions. These people, repositories of special knowledge, had been allowed to testify as "kama'a-ina witnesses." The Richardson Court, accepting the validity and credibility of this practice, saw no reason to discontinue the presentation of such testimony.

19. 54 Hawaii at 176–177, 504 P.2d at 133–134.

20. *McBryde Sugar Co.* v. *Robinson,* 54 Haw. 174 (1973), *rehearing,* 55 Haw. 260, cert. denied, 47 U.S. 976; enforcement enjoined 441 F. Supp. 559 (D. Hawaii 1977).

21. *Honolulu Advertiser,* May 14, 1982.

22. *Robinson* v. *Ariyoshi,* 441 F. Supp. 559 (1977) at 586.

23. *Honolulu Advertiser,* Gerald Kato and Ken Kobayashi, Feb. 20, 1980.

24. 54 Hawaii at 208, 504 P.2d at 1349.

25. *Robinson v. Ariyoshi,* 65 Hawaii 641, 658 P.2d 287, (1982). The associate justices joining in the opinion were Herman Lum and Edward Nakamura, both appointed to the court in 1980; Yoshimi Hayashi, appointed in 1982; and retired justice Benjamin Menor, substituting for disqualified justice Frank Padgett, who also had been appointed in 1982.

The Ninth Circuit's referral of questions to the State High Court had been suggested by the Chief Justice in a "friend of the court" brief submitted by him to the federal court. In his brief and in conversations about the matter, Richardson—displeased that *McBryde* had moved into the federal court system—pointed out that the federal district court would in effect become the appellate court of the State of Hawaii if review by the federal district court was permitted. Also, since there are no time limits on the bringing of challenges to the state court decisions in the federal district courts, the judicial system of the State would be deprived of its most important quality, the ability to resolve any controversy before it with conclusiveness. Brief of Amicus Curiae William S. Richardson, Chief Justice of the Hawaii Supreme Court and Chief Administrator of the Judiciary, State of Hawaii, filed in the U.S. Court of Appeals for the Ninth Circuit.

26. *In re Ashford,* 50 Hawaii 314, 440 P.2d 76 (1968); *County of Hawaii* v. *Sotomura,* 55 Hawaii 176, 517 P.2d (1973); *cert. denied,* 419 U.S. 872 (1973); *In re Sanborn,* 57 Hawaii 585, 562 P.2d 771 (1977); *State* v. *Zimring,* 58 Hawaii 106, 566 P.2d 725 (1977).

27. *Ashford, Sotomura,* and *Sanborn* formed the trio of cases commonly called the shoreline boundary cases.

28. In later years, asked to list the most far-reaching decisions which emanated from the Supreme Court during his years as Chief Justice, Richardson unhesitatingly placed *Ashford* at the top of his list.

29. The common law rejected by *Ashford* did not represent any law established in Hawaii. Rather, the law was applicable to federal lands and most states on the mainland.

30. 50 Hawaii at 315–317, 440 P.2d at 77–78 (Marumoto, J. dissenting).

31. The length of the opinion was the subject of goodnatured jibes from Governor Burns whenever he saw Marumoto over the years to come. Marumoto's explanation for its length was that his opinion might hold meaning for similarly oriented judges in the future. Statement of Masaji Marumoto, in a personal interview, Honolulu, Hawaii, May 21, 1982.

32. 50 Hawaii at 321.

33. *County of Hawaii* v. *Sotomura,* 55 Hawaii 182 (1973).

34. *Sotomura* v. *County of Hawaii,* 402 F. Supp. 95 (D. Haw. 1975)(denial of motion to dismiss); 78-1 Hawaii Legal Reporter at 78–407 (final decision issued October 16, 1978).

35. Cades, J. Russell, "Judicial Legislation in the Supreme Court of Hawaii: A Brief Introduction to the 'Knowne Uncertaintie' of the Law," 7 *Hawaii Bar Journal* 58 (1970).

36. *State* v. *Zimring,* 58 Hawaii 106 (1977). Judge Betty M. Vitousek, temporarily filling a vacancy, wrote a dissenting opinion, raising the question of violation of due process inherent in the taking of private property.

37. Menor's experience was somewhat different in that his birthplace was not Hawaii. Born in the Philippines, he was the first person of Filipino ancestry to be appointed to the Supreme Court. Ogata received his legal training at the University of Michigan, Menor at Boston University. By 1979, Kidwell had retired from the Court and in 1980, Hawaii's Supreme Court was probably the only High Court in the nation without a full-blooded Caucasian.

38. Circuit judge Hiroshi Kato acted as substitute justice in Kidwell's absence.

39. *Yoshizaki* v. *Hilo Hospital,* 50 Hawaii 1 (1967), *rev'd.* 50 Hawaii 150 (1968).

40. See, e.g., *Carvalho* v. *Olim,* 55 Hawaii 335, 519 P.2d 892 (1974); *State* v. *Almeida,* 54 Hawaii 443, 509 P.2d 549 (1973); *State* v. *Santiago,* 53 Hawaii 254, 492 P.2d 657 (1971).

41. See, e.g. *Schwab* v. *Ariyoshi,* 58 Hawaii 25, 555 P.2d 135 (1977); *Life of the Land, Inc.* v. *Land Use Commission,* 61 Hawaii 3, 594 P.2d 1079 (1979).

42. Speech delivered to Hawaiian Civic Club, February 7, 1974, William S. Richardson speech file. See also *Honolulu Advertiser* and *Honolulu Star-Bulletin,* Feb. 14, 1974.

43. Earl Warren and Bill Richardson felt an affinity, Warren making it a point to call Richardson and spend time together whenever he was in Honolulu. The men would drive around the island, ending up at the Richardson beach home at Laie. When Warren was in town at the time of Bebe Richarson's high school graduation, the Richardsons made arrangements for him to attend exercises. The Punahou president stated: "Tickets are at a premium, but how can one deny a seat to the Chief Justice of the United States?!"

44. *Honolulu Advertiser,* Gerald Kato and Ken Kobayashi, Feb. 17, 1980.

45. Holmes, Oliver Wendell, *The Common Law 1 (1881),* Boston: Little, Brown and Company, 1923, p. 1.

46. Statement by William S. Richardson, in a personal interview, Honolulu, Hawaii, Feb. 14, 1984.

Photo Identification
Chapter III, p. 48
Supreme Court justices who issued—from the late 1960s into the 1970s—the controversial land and water decisions, from l. in group picture, Bernard Levinson, Masaji Marumoto, Chief Justice Richardson, Kazuhisa Abe, Bert Kobayashi and from l. below, Benjamin Menor and Thomas Ogata.

"The Chief Justice has played a key role in making the dream of many . . . a reality."

Fujio Matsuda, President, University of Hawaii, 1974–1984
September 2, 1975[1]

"He has done more than any other to make it possible for all of us to be here today."

David Hood, Dean of the Law School, University of Hawaii, 1973–1976
September 2, 1975[2]

"Many young people who would not have had a chance to go to law school . . . are earning positions of leadership."

Richard S. Miller, Dean of the Law School, University of Hawaii, 1982–
October 4, 1982[3]

Stephen Okumura

IV
The Law School

Bill Richardson's childhood, its island textures enhanced and locked into the frieze-frame of memory, fueled his later dreams for establishment of a law school at the University of Hawaii.

Within a few months of becoming Chief Justice, Richardson began to lay plans for a law school. Almost seven years would pass between initial public description of his plans in November, 1966, and convocation ceremonies for Hawaii's first law students.[4] During those seven years, many justifications would be set forth for the law school's formation. While Richardson saw merit in all of them, he retained only one as his central personal motive: fullest opportunities must be given the island youngster who did not have the means to go to the mainland for professional schooling.

This single-minded motive sprang from complexities hidden in an apparently simple childhood. Young Richardson savored the joys unique to a childhood spent on a tropical island, the quintessential paradise. He also absorbed the tensions peculiar to a multi-racial, multi-ethnic, economically polarized community. Once recognized and articulated, these tensions would spur his adult aspirations and achievements.

The Richardsons were not unlike many families in parts of the mainland United States during the 1920s and '30s, when the nation was still predominantly rural, its economic balance unsettled by a depression, its social mores seemingly more defined and less complicated.

When asked about the circumstances of the Chief Justice's childhood, his mother would answer directly, "We were poor, like many other families of our day."

In some cases, being once-poor prods achievement. This was not particularly true of Bill Richardson, for his childhood, though lacking in material comfort, was rich in other respects. He was, after all, descendant of island chiefs, lawyers and judges—a family of some social and professional consequence.

His strong-minded mother—the doer—somehow managed to practice the economies necessary to turn the visions of her husband—the dreamer—into realities. The Chief Justice's later recollections included these economies, but just as strong were pleasurable memories of a time when values and parameters were clear, sense of family and friendship strong.[5]

There usually was not enough money for the family to pay the five-cent trolley fare, so the Richardsons walked everywhere, the boys often carrying a heavy surfboard the two miles to Waikiki from their home in Kaimuki. Bill Richardson later recalled the long walk with surfboard not at all a hardship, but an outing broken by stops for lunch packed by his mother, often of riceballs and sardines; for a snack of dates and cherries picked where the Honolulu Zoo and Kapiolani Park presently stand; for sweet coconut milk and coconut flesh right off the trees in Waikiki, an excess of which he and his friends sometimes sold to tourists.

There was barely enough money for the family's move in 1921 from Palama to Kaimuki and what seemed to them an exorbitantly priced $700 lot in Hawaii's first subdivision. Bill Richardson was a year old at the time. Years after the move, he asked his father why the family had moved from the comfortable ethnic homogeneity of Palama to the racial melting pot of Kaimuki. His father replied: "They raised the rent for our house in Palama from $7 to $8 a month, and I thought *that* was just *too* much!" The house on 5th Avenue in Kaimuki was hammered together of old piano crates which the future Chief Justice's father picked up on the docks. (It was only in 1927 that the family would build a newer, larger house on the same property in front of the house built of crates. Both still stand today.)

The years in a makeshift house continuously renovated and in process of completion were not uncomfortable; they were accepted as part of normal family living. Whatever inconveniences the house afforded, Richardson had other memories of his years there. Wending his way to the house with balloons held carefully, a breathtaking hairline away from overhanging thorned branches along the path.[6] Sharing with neighborhood friends the home and yard space which seemed to expand to accommodate them all.

The Miyamoto family, friends from the old Palama neighborhood whose mother had brought Bill Richardson into the world when the regular midwife could not be found, moved to the Kaimuki area shortly after the Richardsons' move. There, the families continued their close relationship, one which was made even stronger after Mrs. Miyamoto's death. Amy Wung Richardson considered the seven Miyamoto children her own and, in a characteristic gesture, took them wholeheartedly under her wing.

Old Richardson family photographs record picnics, holiday celebrations, sports outings, those family activities which typically were the core of life during the 1920s and '30s. In several of these pictures, still vibrant although faded, the Richardsons and Miyamotos form a center around which other people appear.

What marks these family photos with a difference when

compared to other American family albums of the period is, of course, the Oriental and Hawaiian cast of all of the faces. It is a difference which later acted as catalyst for achievement in many island children, for even in childhood came the realization that powerlessness in Hawaii was very much a matter of race and immigrant status.

Almost inevitably, many island youngsters of the '20s and '30s would work through politics—ethnic politics—to reach for and gain positions of power. And along with their first political stirrings came an increased belief in and reliance upon education as a necessary tool on the path to power.

Amy Wung and Wilfred Richardson knew the importance of education in any people's reach for power, Wilfred all the more sharply because of an educational inadequacy he felt in his own life. Although he completed Normal School teachers' training, an unusual set of circumstances had limited his professional opportunities and had kept him from following the Richardson inclination toward law.

A family occurrence, unusual though not rare, affected Wilfred even before he was born. His father, Colonel John Richardson of Waikapu, Maui, had promised his next son to William Shaw.[7] Shaw, brother of Colonel Richardson's wife, Mary Ann, lived in the then rural area of Lahaina. He was childless himself and, over the years, took in several foster children in the Hawaiian custom of *hanai*.[8]

Compounding Wilfred's sense of being different from his siblings was the fact that he lived in an outlying village, geographically close but psychologically very distant from the relative grandeur of Waikapu, where his blood father held a position of social esteem. Wilfred spoke Hawaiian fluently, English haltingly, and was ridiculed by his three brothers and three sisters as a yokel and an oddity whenever he visited with them.[9]

For a while, Wilfred used Shaw as his surname, reverting back to the Richardson name sometime during his school years at Lahainaluna.

Then, a long illness brought Colonel Richardson's public and professional career to a standstill and, in time, closed off the possibility of higher education for any of his children.[10] Wilfred keenly felt the deprivation. The Richardsons had established a family tradition of accomplishment, and Wilfred—the Richardson who was made to feel that he was not really a Richardson, who thus carried a special onus—was thwarted in his need to continue the tradition.

Adding a subtle dimension to this need, further firing Wilfred's determination to succeed, was the calumny he and his wife suffered in their early years together. Intermarriage between Chinese and Hawaiians—or part-Hawaiians—was rare, and partners in such marriages often were subjected to scorn from both races, neither group willing to concede that the other was its equal.[11]

The ostracism extended to the offspring of these marriages. To be Chinese-Hawaiian, or "*pake*-Hawaiian" in the island idiom, and to be an especially dark skinned *pake*-Hawaiian on top of that, invited taunts from other children. The Richardson youngsters learned at an early age alternately to ignore or to battle the teasing from some of their schoolmates.

The combination of these factors resulting in heightening the ambitions Amy Wung and Wilfred held for themselves and for their children.[12] It also strengthened their recognition that education was a necessary component in fulfillment of those ambitions. Both of them completed teachers' training and spent some years teaching at Makapala School in Kohala on the Big Island before moving to Honolulu.

Another circumstance indirectly fanned the family's desire for success. When the Hawaii National Guard was federalized in 1918, the Richardson family, which then consisted of children Amy and Grace, moved to Schofield Barracks outside of Honolulu so Papa Richardson could serve out his Guard commitment as a second lieutenant. During the year at Schofield, proper quarters and respect accorded an officer whetted the ambitions held by Papa Richardson for a life "better" than his family could enjoy back in Makapala. He and his family elected to remain in Honolulu after completion of his National Guard obligation, renting a home on Hoopili Lane in Palama and busying themselves with the task of educating their children.

Amy Wung, urged by her husband, elected to stay at home while the children were young. "I don't want my children to be running around streets," her husband said, insisting that her presence at home was more important than the extra money they could have had if she continued teaching.[13]

In the Richardsons' view, the best formal education they could afford for their children was to be gotten in Hawaii's public schools, and more specifically, in schools designated as English Standard Schools. In spite of what they perceived as a patronizing attitude toward local children in the establishment of these schools, Amy Wung and Wilfred nonetheless believed that the education there was better than any other within their reach.[14]

English Standard Schools were a logical, yet controversial, development intended to serve many purposes: to deal with the various levels of English language competency in public school students, eventually to minimize differences in mastery; to assuage the desire of native and immigrant parents for the strongest possible education for their children; to gain support for public schools from *haole* middle class parents, many of whom feared the presence of "locals" in the classroom would dilute the quality of their own children's education. Many *haole* parents had no doubt that their culture was dominant because it was superior. What values, they asked, could their children obtain from exposure to the pidgin English spoken by the locals? For that matter, what worthwhile values could be learned from any of the native or immigrant cultures in the islands?

English Standard Schools originated in response to petitions from parents, mostly *haole,* that public schools be developed solely for students who spoke standard English.[15] If that were impossible, parents wanted special public school classes—"sections"—especially earmarked for standard English speakers. In 1924, Hawaii's Department of Public Instruction designated three of its Honolulu schools as English Standard Schools; they soon were followed by three more schools.[16]

These schools had a somewhat similar historical precedent in "select" schools, which began in the mid-1800s and included in their curricula a few classes in English for Hawaiian students. Like "select" schools, English Standard Schools enjoyed a more prestigious reputation than other schools in the public school system, and they created an artificial division which contradicted the notion of equal education for all students.

To the publicly stated purposes for English Standard Schools was added another less-bandied purpose: since agriculture was, and would continue to be, Hawaii's life-blood, a laborer class should not be educated too quickly beyond its station.[17] English Standard Schools or sections, a compromise reasonably acceptable to most island parents, provided a time frame for the "Americanization" of public school students which was deliberate enough to suit Hawaii's sugar planters.[18]

Attempting to solve a terrible dilemma, then, English Standard Schools served a myriad of cross-purposes. But in trying to please everyone, they pleased no one.

Admission for the Standard Schools was based on results of English language proficiency tests. Cursory glance at class rosters of the period quickly shows that although race was not a criterion for admission, few non-*haole*s passed the tests since standard English was spoken in few native and immigrant homes.

Island parents like the Richardsons saw English Standard Schools as a strategem to provide "coolie" education for the poor locals and a more academic education for the *haole* middle class. They were affronted by what they saw as an arbitrary entrance test which would admit Amy, Grace and Bill to Aliiolani Elementary School one year, then deny admission to Arlon and Bobby a few years later; presumably, coming from the same household, their children's mastery of language should have been somewhat parallel.

Businessmen who saw sugar as the islands' most profitable industry were threatened by the knowledge that, in time, students from field laborers' homes would be educated out of their class. Balancing the view of island planters were the mainland-born *haole* professional educators who believed that gradual Americanization of immigrant children through English Standard Schools truly served the students' bests interest.[19] Purposes which the English Standard Schools attempted to serve were complex and, contradicting themselves as they did, would remain clothed in controversy.

In time, the Richardson children would attend Aliiolani Elementary School and Roosevelt High School, both English Standard Schools. They would graduate from the University of Hawaii, and Bill and Robert would go on to the University of Cincinnati for legal training.[20] All his life, Bill Richardson would remain appalled by the discriminatory features of English Standard Schools and never would accept any arguments suggesting their historical necessity. And the memory of the indignities imposed upon non-*haole* students in Hawaii's public school system, one which professed equal opportunity and equal education but delivered neither, would become part of his rationale for a local law school.

Disavowals notwithstanding, the obvious congeniality between the judicial and executive branches almost guaranteed the success of certain projects.

Establishment of a law school was one of these.

Late in 1966, Honolulu newspapers announced the new Chief Justice's desire to establish a law school at the University of Hawaii.[21] That announcement was followed by a spate of actions which suggested seriousness of intent.

No stranger to the idea of winning broad-based support via a cross-section of influential persons, Bill Richardson had appointed fifteen citizens to the Judicial Council shortly after his appointment.[22] The Council, an advisory body to the Supreme Court, had been legislatively-mandated but inactive since 1959. (In the years to come, the Council would instigate any number of projects including law revision, codification, and capital improvements for the courts.) A special subcommittee of the Council was named to examine the possibility of a local law school: members of this subcommittee on Legal Education included Associate Justice Jack Mizuha; Dr. Harold S. Roberts, professor of economics and industrial relations at the University; and Myron Thompson, head of the Liliuokalani Trust, a social service agency established for children of Hawaiian ancestry.

The Chief Justice himself wasted no time in consulting with Hawaii State Bar president William Fleming, and, at the Manoa campus, University president Thomas Hamilton and East-West Center chancellor Howard Jones. Whatever their private reservations may have been, all three publicly supported the idea of a University-connected law school.[23]

In January, 1967, three months after the first newspaper

articles about the law school's possibility, the Chief Justice's Subcommittee on Legal Education presented a report to its parent body. With no hesitation, the Judicial Council accepted the Subcommittee's report and unanimously approved the concept of a law school at the University. Although this action was not a compelling directive in itself, still—coupled with the vocal and enthusiastic support of Council members—it was part of a ripple effect which began to reach an ever-widening audience.[24]

In his 1967 State of the State message to the legislature, Governor Burns—at the behest of the Chief Justice—expressed support of the concept and encouraged legislators to turn that concept into a reality.[25]

While legislative proponents of the law school were in the majority, the concept's acceptance was by no means readily forthcoming.[26] Not surprisingly, members of the bar were among the most vocal in expressing doubts about the project's validity and viability. Would the law school be first rate? Or would it be just a notch above the average trade school, providing training for a vocation rather than education for a profession? Wouldn't monies to be allocated for a law school better be used in scholarships granted to local students for mainland study? Or, shouldn't the University spend these monies to improve existing educational programs unique to Hawaii—in oceanography or tropical agriculture, for example?

Traditionalists, those who revered the kind of legal education obtained at a Harvard Law School, scoffed at the preposterousness of a law school at a state institution like the University of Hawaii. Not even in their wildest imaginings could they conceive of their local University as a Harvard of the West. Others believed that an academically sound law school could be established at the University. Besides providing legal education for local students who could not otherwise obtain it, the school could serve many other purposes: as a base for continuing legal education; as a center for comparative legal studies in Pacific-basin trade and international relations; as a research institute for examination of problems unique to an island state once an island kingdom.

The University of Hawaii sent to the Governor, the legislature, and University faculty members its own informal findings on the possibility of a law school. While generally favorable to establishment of a law school, the University report cited the need for a more detailed follow-up evaluation.[27] Such an evaluation, response to a request from the 1967 Legislature for a comprehensive law school feasibility study, eventually would begin in December, 1968, and end in March, 1969.[28] The Warren-Mearns report, as some called it, was the result of efforts spearheaded by Chief Justice Richardson.

The Chief Justice and his Judicial Council had not been idle on the law school question during 1967 and 1968, garnering support wherever they could.[29] Realizing that their efficacy would be increased with additional help from others, particularly from those in positions of political leadership, Council members decided to invite several non-Council persons to augment their Subcommittee on Legal Education: Senator George Ariyoshi and Representative Stuart Ho, Democrat leaders in the legislature; Senator Hebden Porteus, Republican leader; Richard Schulze, an attorney; and C. Frank Damon, Jr., president of the Bar Association in 1968.[30]

Meanwhile, Chief Justice Richardson consulted with national leaders in law education, usually by telephone, sometimes in connection with trips he took to organize what would become eventually the National Center for State Courts. With the help of Frank Damon and Dr. Harold Roberts, he also looked into the possibility of funding from foundations to subsidize a feasibility study. In November, 1968, Dean William C. Warren of the Columbia University School of Law and Professor Edward A. Mearns, Jr., of the Northwestern School of Law agreed to begin work on the feasibility study. In March, 1969, the local McInerny Foundation deposited $6,250 with the University of Hawaii Foundation for study-related expenses.[31]

The Warren-Mearns study, presented in March to the 1969 Legislature, substantiated the case for a law school. It cited statistics demonstrating that national and local population growth would result in an increased demand for attorneys. It described the many services that the school could provide the community, such as serving as a center for research, reform, and continuing legal education. Finally, it projected a scenario for plant and program development from September, 1969 to June, 1977, with the first class slated for September, 1972.[32]

Debate on the merits of a local law school continued through 1969 and 1970. During its 1970 session, the legislature once again heard testimony for and against formation of a local law school.[33] University President Cleveland envisioned a school of an "innovative" nature which would "burst out of tradition."[34] Others pictured a school of a more conventional nature.

Governor Burns continued to make his influence felt in many ways, quietly working with legislators behind the scenes, publicly supporting law school formation in speeches.[35] Even though together Burns and Richardson were formidable persuaders, cautious legislators recommended in May, 1970, that another study be conducted. The new study, this time legislatively-funded, would determine community support, examine alternative types of schools that might be established, and provide a cost-benefit analysis for a local school.[36] Directed by the legislature to conduct the study, the Legislative Reference Bureau contracted the work to Norman Meller, a University of Hawaii political science professor.

In the meantime, in a separate development, University President Cleveland announced to his Board of Regents that Bayless Manning and Thomas Ehrlich, respectively dean and professor at the Stanford Law School, would conduct a cost-benefit analysis in the fall of 1970. The Ehrlich-Manning report was circulated to interested groups throughout the community for feedback.[37] The University later incorporated ideas generated by the report into a publication describing legal education programs to be instituted at the University of Hawaii.[38]

Both the Warren-Mearns report and the Ehrlich-Manning report provided a base for the Meller report, released early in 1971.[39] While points of emphasis varied, the overall tone of all three reports were positive enough that in May of the same year, the legislature—with very few dissenters—established and provided appropriations for a law school at the University.[40]

In September, 1973, the University of Hawaii inaugurated its law school, and Chief Justice Richardson and David R. Hood, the school's new dean, untied the symbolic *maile* fern *lei* for fifty-three first-class students.

Obtaining legislative mandate for the law school was only the first hurdle. Other problems would erupt periodically over the next decade, twice—in 1975 and 1979—with such vigor that the very existence of the new institution seemed threatened.[41]

In addition to the normal growing pains of any young educational venture, the law school faced some unusual obstacles. One of these was a thinly veiled hostility from many practicing lawyers, some of whom were in the State legislature. The school also suffered from an identity crisis which involved clashes between "locals" and outsiders, as well as between one group which wanted a strong academic reputation for their school and another which believed that to stress traditional scholarship would contradict a prime reason for the school's creation. This second group asked: How could the school impose strict and conventional academic requirements if one of its purposes was to serve a class of youngsters historically denied a first rate education?

The question of academic standards was discussed in relation to two issues: a pre-admission program initiated at the law school in 1974 and a pass rate for the State bar examination which increased steadily over the years. The pre-admission program provided extra help to disadvantaged students in ethnic categories underrepresented in the State bar, primarily those students who were Samoan, Filipino, or Hawaiian. Besides eight credits of regular first year classes, the pre-admission students took a three-credit introductory law course which included analysis and legal writing. A C-average (a 2 on a 4-point scale) over a two-year period elevated the student to a regular status.[42] Law school skeptics viewed the need for this program as proof that scholarship in the law school was less than top notch.

The Chief Justice agreed that educational deficiencies which resulted from minority status needed active correction and he gave more than token support for the pre-admission program. He personally followed the academic progress of Hawaiian and part-Hawaiian students at the school, meeting with any and all who wished to see him, offering words of advice and encouragement whenever he could.[43]

In speaking to Hawaiian groups, the Chief Justice constantly reported on the progress of Hawaiian students in the law school and in the legal community. Richardson always made it clear that Hawaiians could work for desired changes from within the system. He expressed these feelings explicitly in a 1977 speech:

> Until recently, Hawaiians have tended to stay outside the legal system because we did not understand the law and the courts. We watched in frustration as our lands were lost to us under laws which were completely foreign to the ancient Hawaiian concepts of land ownership, and we saw our people made liable for 'crimes' that did not exist under the old Hawaiian system. I know that some of you may disagree with me, but I believe we must accept the fact that we live under a system of laws and courts, which have replaced the traditional ways of our ancestors, and, in order to preserve our people, culture, and land, we must take an active role in this system. The law can be used by creative attorneys as a sword for advancing the rights of our Hawaiian people.[44].

Richardson's desire to widen educational and professional avenues for local students spilled over into other areas: the Chief Justice advocated generous Supreme Court policies governing the bar exam, policies which often exasperated attorney-examiners who wished to apply more stringent standards of admission to the State bar. A 1978 newspaper article commented on the bar examination's steadily rising pass rate which consistently placed Hawaii ahead of the national average during the decade that Bill Richardson had been Chief Justice. From an average pass rate of 51% from statehood in 1959 to 1966, the pass rate average increased to 83% in the next decade under Richardson's stewardship, with 91% of the examinees passing the test in 1978.[45]

Not only were some of the attorney-examiners exasperated, most of the Bar was extremely concerned. Bill Richardson brushed off the objections as understandably apprehensive statements: why *should* any practicing lawyer want to share the pie with any more persons than necessary? The Chief Justice, who—as his opponents were quick to remind others—had never himself taken the bar, believed that the bar exam was a mere formality. He would have eliminated it altogether had not law school deans across the nations convinced him otherwise. Richardson maintained that anyone who could meet and pass the challenges during three years at an accredited law school was more than equipped to practice law: "Let the consumers determine a lawyer's success; let the marketplace be the final arbiter."[46]

The Chief Justice correctly believed that the Supreme Court's responsibility in the matter was to admit competent lawyers to the bar, not to regulate their flow to please the legal community. But the *degree* of competency was an issue in the argument between Richardson and many practicing attorneys whose position was stated by the State Bar Association's leadership. And by too quickly assigning self-protection as the sole motive of the Association, the Chief Justice failed to hear the voices of those individual lawyers who took genuine pride in their profession and who were truly concerned about the degree of competency displayed by persons admitted to the Bar.

Typifying such attorneys was Daniel Case, president of the Hawaii State Bar Association in 1978. Case responded to the Chief Justice's position, saying that he did not believe his Association's primary goal was to limit the number of qualified lawyers in Hawaii: "That sort of guild approach is not held by too many people. There is always room for qualified people." Case added that with growing numbers of law school graduates in Hawaii and through the nation, the "test of quality" should be kept "intact"; moreover, that test would be an important means for the University of Hawaii law school to show that the training it provided was strong.[47]

Academic standards and differing philosophies held by "locals" versus "outsiders" were only two issues which needed resolution as the law school established its identity. Other impediments in the law school's path to respectability and acceptance were the intertwined problems of a turnover of deans, inadequate facilities, and a lack of a permanent site. Combined, these factors affected granting of permanent accreditation by the American Bar Association.

The turnover of deans and the question of an adequate level of instructors were partly caused by a low salary schedule coupled with high living costs in Hawaii. Another part of the problem was what some observers described obliquely as "unwarranted meddling in academic affairs" on the part of some University regents and administrators.[48] Privately, persons close to the situation implied or said outright that the regents and administration—influenced by the outspoken champion of island "locals," Wally Fujiyama—busied themselves too much with school-related details that were the rightful province of the dean and his faculty.[49]

David Hood, who served as the school's first dean from 1973 until the first class' graduation in 1976, was credited with establishing sound curricular and operational foundations against great difficulties.[50] Hood was followed by Clifford Thompson, who became dean in January, 1977, and left in August of the following year, when professor Jerome Dupont was named as interim dean and a search was conducted for yet another dean.[51]

The search was complicated by a number of factors. A well-known dean would help attract strong faculty and students, yet such a person probably would not consider a post where the salary was low, where a high measure of political sensitivity and skill seemed necessary, and where permanent accreditation did not appear imminent.

Finally, Marvin J. Anderson, distinguished dean and chancellor at University of California's Hastings College of Law, decided to take a temporary leave from Hastings. In January, 1980, he took on the Hawaii post as interim dean and legal education assistant to the chancellor. Anderson's assignment was explicit and twofold: first, to examine the curriculum; second, to find a site and lay plans for permanent physical facilities.

The law school's temporary quarters were in the University quarry, an area of makeshift buildings serving a hodge-podge of functions: parking, athletics, ROTC, and home economics.

A number of amazingly diverse sites were suggested for permanent facilities: in the downtown area, either the Old Federal Building or a new law-related complex of buildings; in the University area, either an elementary school in Manoa with a dwindling enrollment, or the space above the multideck parking structure in the University quarry. At last, legislative appropriations for law school construction was made in 1980, and actual construction was begun in March, 1981.

The initial stages of actual construction were not without their problems, either. The 1981 appropriations were earmarked for a three-building complex—classrooms, library, and administrative offices—to be located on the top level of the parking deck in the quarry. Instead, the contractor laid foundations for the library at a Dole Street location close to the legislatively-approved site. When later asked about the change in plans, both the University president and the State comptroller replied that reviews of plans by a structural engineer disclosed that the library was too heavy to be placed on top of the parking floors. To delay construction at the Dole Street site for a year in order to obtain legislative approval would have added millions of dollars to building costs; both men said that they realized their decision to proceed without approval was a "gamble," but a "gamble" which would save the State some $6.1 million in cost overrun.[52] Construction was allowed to proceed at the Dole Street location.

The lack of a permanent building was one obstacle in the

law school's pursuit of permanent accreditation. The lack of a permanent dean was another. Having completed his assignment of reviewing the curriculum, securing a permanent site, and overseeing initial phases of facilities construction at the law school, interim dean Anderson stepped aside in 1981 when the search for a permanent dean began.[53]

In 1974, a year after the law school opened its doors to the first students, the American Bar Association (ABA) had awarded the school provisional accreditation on the basis of a report by its evaluation team.

The following year, the law school was subjected to three more evaluation studies. The first was conducted by the ABA accreditation committee which, as a matter of policy, examines provisionally-accredited institutions on a yearly basis. The second was conducted by a "Committee of Visitors," a group of five local lawyers appointed by the University of Hawaii president. The third 1975 study was conducted by the Hawaii State legislature.

Although all three studies complimented the law school, no amount of praise could camouflage the absence of a dean or of permanent facilities. Other deficiencies were equally obvious: a shortage of full-time faculty members; an inadequate library; salary deficiencies.

With the naming of Richard S. Miller as law school dean in July, 1982, with staff additions, increase in library volumes, ongoing construction of permanent facilities, the obstacles to permanent accreditation fell away one by one.[54] At its August, 1982 meeting in San Francisco, the ABA's House of Delegates voted unanimously to grant full accreditation to the eight-year old law school at the University of Hawaii.

In 1980, in the face of problems which threatened the law school's existence, several students appeared before the legislature to ask for continued support. Legislators would decide to heed their pleas and continue to fund their institution. The students' collective testimony in part described who they were: "We are not sons and daughters of doctors, real estate tycoons, professors or bankers. . . . Most of us are the first in our families to pursue a college education."[55]

What more visible proof that Richardson's prime reason for wanting a law school was valid and well-served?

---

1. *Honolulu Advertiser,* Sep. 3, 1975.

2. *Ibid.*

3. *Honolulu Star-Bulletin,* A. A. Smyser, Oct. 4, 1982.

4. Richardson publicly announced his plans through interviews with news reporters. *Honolulu Advertiser,* Drew McKillips, Nov. 15, 1966; *Honolulu Star-Bulletin,* Harriet Gee, Nov. 15, 1966.

5. One wonders at Amy Wung Richardson's ability to create such a sense of family. In spite of—perhaps because of—her father's death when she was only three months old, she became an unusually forceful parent figure. Amy Wung was the youngest of eight children born to Chinese Christian immigrants, her mother having travelled to Hawaii as picture bride to "a good man" some twenty to twenty-five years her senior. Statement of Amy Wung Richardson in interviews conducted for the Chinese History Center by Dorothy Soong and Sybil Ho on September 2, 1971, and a conversation with Jane Silverman on May 24, 1978.

6. The Chief Justice's mother reminisced about those early Kaimuki days just before her death in 1980: "There was hardly anyone there when we moved there. It was just a dirt lane through the trees. I remember on balloon days we would go to Liberty House and when the children came home with the balloons they would get punctured on the *kiawe* thorns before we got home and the children would all cry, especially Bill." *Ibid.*

7. Colonel Richardson's title derived from the fact that he was Knight Commander to King Kalakaua.

8. One of Wilfred's daughters, Grace, tells a family story about the circumstances of Wilfred's *hanai* adoption. Apparently, Colonel Richardson forgot to tell his wife of his promise to Shaw. When she learned of the promise, Mary Ann Richardson stubbornly refused to give up her infant.

Shaw was persistent and one day simply abducted the child. Periodically, Mary Ann would tell the tale of how her brother "kidnapped" her baby Wilfred. Statement of Grace Richardson Wong, in an interview with Scott Shirai, Honolulu, Hawaii, Dec. 20, 1982.

9. Wilfred's daughter, Grace, relates a story illustrating her father's continued mixed attitudes toward the Hawaiian language. Feeling both pride and shame about his mother's native language, Wilfred early decided to subordinate its importance to English, whose mastery he felt was necessary if one were to succeed in Hawaii's multi-ethnic society. He impressed his English-language bias upon his children with such vigor that when Grace, the recipient of a Danforth Fellowship, went to the mainland and was called upon to address her fellow students with a few words of Hawaiian, the *only* word she could muster up from her memory was "Aloha." *Ibid.*

10. Colonel Richardson, felled by a stroke for the last eleven years of his life, spent some of that time in Leahi, a convalescent home in Honolulu for consumptives and a few patients with other health problems.

11. Whenever asked, Amy Wung Richardson would describe frankly the prejudices she, her husband, and her children suffered at the hands of both the Chinese and Hawaiian communities. She recalled that she was only the third or fourth Chinese girl in her community to marry a Hawaiian: "Everyone told me he'll be a drunkard and no good. The Hawaiians where we lived never worked, they just went fishing all day. . . . My husband was a kind man. He said, 'Never mind, I'll take care of you.' They told me my children would be lazy and they would be black." Soong, Ho, and Silverman, *op. cit.*

12. To have one son become a lawyer, one a doctor, and one a minister did not seem far-fetched goals to Wilfred. "I want one to hang 'em, one to pronounce 'em dead, and one to bury 'em," he would say in a joking, yet serious way. Bill was to be the lawyer and judge, Robert the doctor, and Arlon the minister. Robert did begin pre-med studies before deciding to join Bill in the study of law; Arlon became an engineer. Statement by Arlon Richardson, in an interview with Scott Shirai, Honolulu, Hawaii, Dec. 18, 1982.

13. It was not until Robert, the youngest child, was three or four years old and "times got hard" that Amy Wung returned to the teaching profession at Castle Kindergarten, where she remained until it was disbanded towards the end of World War II. Soong, Ho, and Silverman, *op. cit.* She later taught at Mother Rice School in Moiliili for many more years, all the while actively involved in volunteer community projects.

14. Although later, the Chief Justice courteously would say that the Richardson children could not afford to go to the Kamehameha Schools, costs at Princess Bernice Pauahi Bishop's school were not much more than public school costs coupled with at-home room and board expenses. Amy Wung and Wilfred Richardson simply preferred the education available at English Standard Schools, disliking the vocational emphases they saw at Kamehameha.

15. MacCaughey, Vaughan, to Governor Charles J. McCarthy, July 1, 1920, Archives of Hawaii.

16. Lincoln, Roosevelt, Stevenson, Aliiolani, Jefferson and Kapalama Schools were designated as English Standard Schools in Honolulu. Shortly afterwards, one school each on the Big Island of Hawaii, Maui, and Molokai were given such designation. English Standard sections were established in schools located in less populated areas. Although implementation of the English Standard Schools concept began in 1924, it was not until 1927 that the Territorial Legislature officially directed the DPI to establish these schools and sections.

17. A report known as the Prosser Report best presents this point of view, albeit in such an extreme form that it offended even some of the islands' staunchest industrialists. Written by Charles A. Prosser of Minneapolis' Dunwoody Industrial Institute at the behest of local businessmen, the Report predictably praised vocational training, pointed out the folly of overeducating youth, and left no doubt that education should be handmaiden to King Sugar. Governor's Advisory Committee on Education, *Survey of Schools and Industry* (Honolulu: J. K. Butler, 1930–31).

18. Not until 1949 would legislation be passed requiring a gradual increase in Standard sections so that all public schools in time would be converted to one standard; this finally occurred in the early 1960s.

19. Some of these educators, such as David L. Crawford, could not conceive any other than agricultural supremacy in the islands. Regretting the clash between development of education and development of the sugar industry, Crawford proposed work-study solutions accommodating both. David L. Crawford, *Paradox in Hawaii: An Examination of Industry and Education and the Paradox They Present* (Boston: The Stratford Co., 1933).

20. Dr. Leonora N. Bilger, Bill's chemistry professor at the University of Hawaii, influenced the Richardson brothers' enrollment at the University of Cincinnati, where she had earned her undergraduate and graduate degrees. A respected and indefatigable educator, the reach of her work and

influence was wide-ranging. After completion of law school and return to the islands, Bill in turn directed his friend Wally Fujiyama to the University of Cincinnati.

21. *Honolulu Advertiser,* Drew McKillips, Nov. 15, 1966; *Honolulu Star Bulletin,* Harriet Gee, Nov. 15, 1966. Actually, the first public statements about the possibility of a local law school appear to have been made by Hawaii's Republican Governor William F. Quinn in 1960. *Honolulu Star Bulletin,* Sep. 3, 1960.

22. The Chief Justice served as the Council's chairman. Members appointed to staggered three-year terms included attorney J. Russell Cades; attorney Walter G. Chuck; Circuit Judge Masato Doi; the Rev. Claude F. Du Teil; government administrator Arthur Hoke; businessman-politician Richard Lyman, Jr.; Boyd McNaughton, president of C. Brewer & Co.; Masaji Marumoto, Supreme Court Associate Justice, 1956–60 and 1967–73; Supreme Court Associate Justice Jack Mizuha; attorney Hideki Nakamura; businessman Stanley Powell, Jr.; Dr. Harold S. Roberts, chairman, University of Hawaii's department of business and economics; Myron Thompson, director at Liliuokalani Trust; attorney Betty Vitousek; Associate Justice Cable A. Wirtz.

23. *Honolulu Advertiser,* Drew McKillips, Nov. 15, 1966.

24. Decisions of the Judicial Council, whose assigned function was merely advisory, carried no legal clout. The Council's power lay in the individual and collective abilities of its members to inform, persuade, and motivate others in the community; over the years, the efficacy of the Council varied, depending in great part on the influence, the interest and energy level of its members.

25. Address by Governor John A. Burns, Joint Session, Fourth State Legislature, General Session of 1967, Legislative Reference Bureau. Education was a priority in the Democrats' vision of a "New Hawaii," so many of the young Democrat leaders recognizing the value of education in their own rise to power. Besides specifically calling for a law school feasibility study in his 1967 address, Gov. Burns repeated his party's commitment to education: ". . . as in the past the primary emphasis in our recommended budgets lies in the area of improved educational services and facilities, carrying forward our program toward achieving excellence in education."

26. In 1963, the *Star-Bulletin* had run an article containing views that a cross-section of citizens, most of them lawyers and judges, held toward establishment of a local law school. Very few expressed enthusiastic support. *Honolulu Star-Bulletin,* Jan. 8, 1963.

27. *Honolulu Star-Bulletin,* Feb. 29, 1968.

28. The evaluation was a reply to HR 284, a request for a comprehensive law school feasibility study.

29. The Council's composition had altered slightly by the end of 1968. Associate Justice Wirtz had resigned early in 1967; his place on the Council was filled by businessman Hung Wo Ching in June. Associate Justice Mizuha's resignation early in 1968 resulted in Associate Justice Kazuhisa Abe's appointment to the Council.

30. Damon, who believed that a local school could serve the local bar's need for continuing education, was unable to convince his board to issue an endorsement for the school; nevertheless, Damon himself announced personal endorsement whenever he could. A year after his presidency, the Bar Association was willing to go only as far as publicly supporting the legislature's call for a feasibility study. Information from files on Law School and general correspondence, office of William S. Richardson.

31. Although three bills calling for feasibility study appropriations were introduced during the 1969 legislative session—SB 300, HB 630, and HB 897—none of them got very far. Legislative Reference Bureau, Honolulu, Hawaii. Of the McInerny funds, $4813.76 was unused and returned to the McInerny Foundation. Statement of Lois Loomis, Bishop Trust officer, in a telephone conversation, March 4, 1983.

32. Warren, William C., and Mearns, Edward A., Jr., "The School of Law, University of Hawaii: Its Feasibility and Social Importance," March, 1969.

33. In addition to carryover bills from the previous session, two more bills specifically relating to law school formation were introduced—HB 1339, HB 1504; again, none of the bills passed. Legislative Reference Bureau, Honolulu, Hawaii.

34. *Honolulu Advertiser,* Feb. 13, 1970.

35. In a 1970 speech to the Young Lawyers Section of the Bar, for instance, Burns declared that the University would have both a law school and a medical school within four years. *Honolulu Advertiser,* September 5, 1970. The University's medical school became a *bona fide* four year institution in 1973; it was named for Governor Burns shortly before his death in 1975.

36. Although measures specifically relating to the law school were not passed by the 1970 Legislature, HB 1160-70, a general revenues appropriations bill, was passed; it contained funds allocated for a law school feasibility study.

37. Ehrlich, Thomas and Manning, Thomas, "Programs in Law at the

University of Hawaii: A Report to the President of the University," Honolulu, Hawaii, Dec. 1970.

38. Cleveland, Harlan and Heyman, I. Michael, "Programs in Legal Education at the University of Hawaii," University of Hawaii, Honolulu, Hawaii, Jan. 1972.

39. Meller, Norman, "Hawaii Law School Study," Legislative Reference Bureau Report No. 3, University of Hawaii, Honolulu, Hawaii, 1971. The reported estimated costs of $3,460,000 to construct a law school building and $500,000 to assemble a law library.

40. HB 93-71 became Act 146. The Act provided $192,500 for the law school during fiscal biennium 1971–73.

41. *Honolulu Star-Bulletin,* Feb. 5, 1975; *Honolulu Advertiser,* Dec. 19, 1979.

42. The 1978 Bakke "reverse discrimination" decision rendered by the U.S. Supreme Court caused some modification in the U.H. Law School's pre-admission program. In the summer of 1978, two Caucasian women who had been denied entrance to the U.H. graduate school and one who had been rejected by the U.H. Law School asked the American Civil Liberties Union to represent them, claiming that they were penalized by admission policies which favored minority students.

43. Certain students grew so close to him that they periodically paid *en masse* visits to the Chief Justice in his chambers; they also planned occasional discussion weekends at his beachhouse in Laie.

44. June 24, 1977 speech, William S. Richardson speech file, Honolulu, Hawaii.

45. These figures were based upon data available in "The Bar Examiner," an American Bar Association-affiliated publication. *Honolulu Advertiser,* James Dooley, Nov. 27, 1978.

46. Statement by William S. Richardson, in an interview, Honolulu, Hawaii, June 30, 1982.

47. *Honolulu Advertiser,* James Dooley, Nov. 27, 1978.

48. *Honolulu Advertiser,* Nov. 14, 1975.

49. Statements made in confidence by a number of persons, in a series of interviews, Honolulu, Hawaii, 1982. See also *Honolulu Advertiser,* Aug. 16, 1975; Nov. 28, 1975, for generalized description of the situation.

50. Hood, a native of Tacoma Washington and a graduate of Harvard Law School, for a while practiced in Seattle, then taught at Wayne State University when tapped for the deanship.

51. Thompson, a graduate of Harvard Law School and a Rhodes scholar at Magdalen College, Oxford, arrived in Hawaii from a decade in

legal education in Africa and then a teaching post at Southern Methodist University. Dupont, who came from the University of Michigan to the law school as assistant professor and law librarian in 1976, also served as interim dean for a few months between Hood and Thompson.

52. *Honolulu Star-Bulletin,* April 29, 1981.

53. Once Anderson completed his duties with the law school, he was named interim chancellor at the University of Hawaii in September, 1981, then chancellor in July, 1982.

54. Miller, acting associate dean in 1976–77 and interim dean since October of 1981, had been at the law school since its beginning. He attended Yale and Boston University law schools, taught at the Wayne State University Law School, and was law school professor and administrator at Ohio State University before joining the law faculty at the University of Hawaii.

55. *Honolulu Star-Bulletin,* Helen Altonn, Feb. 12, 1980.

Photo Identification
Chapter IV, p. 82
The first class to graduate, in 1976, from the UH law school, later to be named the William S. Richardson School of Law.

"I think every person has a special contribution to make. It's part of my job to find the proper place for him."

William S. Richardson, Chief Justice, Hawaii Supreme Court
February 11, 1982[1]

" 'The difficult we do immediately. The impossible takes a little longer.' "

Lester E. Cingcade, Administrative Director of the Courts
June 8, 1982[2]

"Maybe Les and I work so well with each other for The Boss because we are so unalike."

Tom "Fat Boy" Okuda, Deputy Director of the Courts
April 7, 1983[3]

V
Court Administration

When Bill Richardson became Chief Justice in 1966, he knew that his two broad constitutional mandates were to be chief lawmaker and chief administrator of Hawaii's court system. He had only a vague notion of his specific duties.

He describes those days with candor: "I was reminded of my earliest days as chief clerk in the 1955 and 1957 Territorial Senate. None of us Democrats had any first-hand exposure to the legislative process; the Republicans had been in power so long and we had been on the outs since the beginning of time. It was a matter of guess, bluff, just do, and hope that *something* would be right!"

Richardson smiles at the memory of those early moments in the Supreme Court courtroom: "The other justices were Republicans. A few of them had been hoping for the chief justiceship themselves and I'm sure they wanted to see me fall on my face. But they were very kind, quietly pointing out what I was doing wrong in the courtroom. On the administrative front, Les Cingcade was learning to become my strong right arm."

That was in 1966.

By 1982, the administrative achievements of the Richardson years on the bench had been considerable. A 1983 management analysis of Hawaii's court system done by the National Center for State Courts, an independent research and advisory body, commended Hawaii's system beyond normal expectations.

A negative report would have been surprising, given that Hawaii's courts periodically had won praise from a number of national figures and agencies as a model system. In addition, Bill Richardson was an incorporating director of the Center since 1971, its president in 1980, and he had maintained ties with Center staff of unusual closeness and longevity.

Being an incorporating director meant that for months in 1971, Richardson made many weekend trips to the eastern U.S., usually Washington, D.C., to meet with other state chief justices and U.S. Chief Justice Warren E. Burger, who—with the support of his President Richard M. Nixon—conceived and announced the idea of a national center to serve state courts in March, 1971.[4] Hawaii's ties with the National Center certainly would predispose center staff toward a favorable analysis of Hawaii's courts. But even with this predisposition, there was no denying the accomplishments which led the Center to label Hawaii's court system as "progressive and dynamic."[5]

In its report, the Center pointed out that Hawaii was the only state to commission an evaluation by an outside agency, added proof of its progressivism. The Center praised Hawaii's march toward independence away from the executive and legislative branches. Milestones in this march included development of a budgetary system free from executive control in 1974 and a totally self-contained personnel system in 1977. Independence was further confirmed by creation of disciplinary mechanisms for lawyers and judges: for lawyers, the Disciplinary Board of the

Supreme Court in 1973; and for judges, the Commission on Judicial Discipline in 1979. The High Court's rule-making power for all State courts solidified judicial independence even more.

An adjunct and auxiliary development was unification of various court functions. Although the State courts in four judicial circuits sprawled through most of the eight-island chain, strong, centralized authority was placed in the offices of the chief justice and administrative director at Honolulu, Hawaii's capital city and historical focal point. This administrative model proved efficient and cost-effective.

In 1966, the Family Court Act brought together the once separate juvenile and domestic relations courts under one roof and one philosophy. In the same year, Hawaii's Supreme Court Law Library was established as a statewide library. In addition, responsibility for the district courts shifted from county to state government, unifying all courts into a single system which served the entire State. In 1972, the district courts became courts of record with direct lines of appeal to the Supreme Court rather than through the circuit courts for purposes of establishing record; consolidation of the twenty-seven district court divisions into four jurisdictions with the same geographic boundaries as the circuit courts additionally streamlined Hawaii's system.

Another organizational change was the creation in 1980 of a three-judge intermediate court of appeals, a court for which Richardson had lobbied vigorously during the 1978 Constitutional Convention. Richardson's action during the Convention was seen as somewhat atypical action for a chief justice, but he was convinced that an intermediate court would ease appellate backlog. Also, he felt that his assignment as chief court administrator justified his involvement in any action would lead to administrative improvements.

His campaign for an intermediate court actually began

several years before the Convention and, at many points during those years, was a solely personal effort, fueled only by Richardson's persistence. Judiciary personnel marvelled at his perseverance in this effort: "Ordinary mortals would have given up, the obstacles seemed so numerous."[6]

Richardson's campaign began informally as he spoke with judges from other states during the many meeting and conferences he attended on the mainland. Having identified trial court delay as his major administrative problem in his earliest days on the bench and having alleviated that problem through series of minor procedural changes, he then had turned his attention to the problem of appellate delay.[7] His discussions with intermediate appellate judges seemed to follow similar patterns: almost unanimously, those judges stated that in their respective states, initial public reaction to a new intermediate appellate level was negative; then, after a few months, those negative feelings changed and the intermediate courts began to be viewed as an essential and important part of the judicial system.

Richardson formally began his campaign for an intermediate appellate court in Hawaii in his annual State of the Judiciary address to the Hawaii Bar in November, 1976. The idea was mentioned briefly in the text of his speech, presented in a very low-keyed and diplomatic way. When the 1977 State Legislature convened in January, on legislators' desks was a Judiciary bill intended to create an appellate division of the State's circuit courts. That bill died, as Richardson had supposed it would, but served its purpose of centering public and legislative attention on the possibility of an appellate level in Hawaii's court system.

Richardson had asked the National Center to conduct a study on the desirability of an intermediate appellate court for Hawaii. The Center's preliminary report to him advised against such a court. Undaunted, Richardson persuaded the

Center that its recommendation was superficial, and he asked for another more "complete" study. His own staff members, perhaps reacting instinctively to Richardson's conviction that the recommendation was wrong, somehow "lost" the Center's preliminary findings in their files. They later claimed that Richardson's prestige and power at the National Center was responsible for the turnabout in its final, more "complete" recommendation urging formation of an intermediate court of appeals in Hawaii.[8] Attempting to cover as many bases as possible, the Chief Justice then expressed his sentiments for an intermediate appellate court in a *Hawaii Bar Journal* article.[9] At about the same time, he asked his Judicial Council to discuss suggested court administration changes contained in a package he himself would present at the Constitutional Convention. Hoping for council endorsement of every change, the Chief Justice was disappointed when Council members decided on a course of neutrality; nevertheless, once again, Council discussion of the proposed changes raised public awareness about an intermediate appellate court, one of the items in the package.

Lobbying for the Intermediate Court of Appeals at the Convention was not easy. The Hawaii State Bar Association was against such a court and once again, Daniel Case, Bar president in 1978, presented a view which opposed Richardson's: "The creation of an intermediate appellate court represents a radical change from the existing judicial system. The bar association believes that an intermediate court would add expense to the judicial system, without any improvement in the judicial system." Richardson insisted: "Such a court is an inevitable institutional reform, not a radical action." The Bar favored increasing the number of justices and establishing three-member panels to hear appeals; Richardson thought this a "band-aid setup."[10]

The Convention eventually approved Richardson's plan

and Hawaii would replicate the experience of other states in gaining public acceptance of its Intermediate Court of Appeals.

Within a decade after Richardson had become chief justice, Hawaii's Judiciary had assumed the salient features and advantages of a unified, corporate structure: efficiency through centralization, reduced duplication, uniform standards and procedures.

Apart from an organizational structure that worked well, the National Center's 1982 management analysis praised Hawaii's innovative spirit, citing experimentation with and adoption of court technology as an example. A computer systems office had been established in 1974 with federal monies and was assigned the task of careful, systematic development of computerized systems within the State Judiciary. By 1982, several court functions were successfully computerized. These included a traffic violations system for Oahu; a statewide jury selection and jury payroll system; and a master index of cases in the First Judicial Circuit, the State's largest circuit encompassing Oahu and part of Molokai.

Hawaii's innovative bent also exhibited itself in an early reach into the community for purposes of communication. In 1967 and 1972, two statewide Judiciary-sponsored public conferences provided a forum of exchange for court staff, professionals in related fields, and interested citizenry. The courts' volunteer program began on a formal basis in 1971, with volunteers providing one-to-one companionship for clients identified in Family Court and adult probation programs. Gradually it expanded until there were volunteer counterparts for nearly every court staff position. By the late 1970s volunteers were providing in-kind services which yearly amounted to at least a hundred thousand dollars. Perhaps it was his prior political background which gave Richardson a keen sense of what private citizens could contribute as volunteers. His frequent statements in support and appreciation of volunteerism both sustained volunteer regulars and attracted new helpers to the Judiciary.

A final example of Hawaii's pioneering approach, according to the National Center's report, was its adoption of a long range planning document in 1981. The first of its kind in the nation, the document established procedures for statewide court employee participation in defining and implementing future directions for the Judiciary.[11]

Of course, the link between financial resources of the Hawaii State Judiciary and its modern, forward-looking orientation was more than casual. To be progressive, an institution needs money, and many State Capitol onlookers claimed that the Judiciary had few equals when it came to claiming the legislative dollar.

Chief Justice Richardson, his administrative director Les Cingcade, and his deputy director Tom Okuda were a fascinating triumvirate, an almost classic case study of different personalities united by common goals. Their end goal, of course, was a modern, effective, efficiently-run Judiciary. However, they were realistic enough to know that their best plans had no hope of success without legislative funding; developing clout at the legislature was, therefore, a crucial first goal.

Richardson's position dictated that he remain somewhat aloof from the business of fund-raising. But his politician's instinct for mobilizing people and orchestrating plans, even from a distance, did not fail him or the Judiciary. He nurtured cordial relations with most legislators, especially key legislators. ("No, no, you visited me in my chambers last time. I'll come to *your* Capitol office this time.") Cingcade, a former teacher and school administrator originally from Eagle Point, Oregon, was responsible for translating the

Chief Justice's directives into day-to-day operations; it was he, with his pragmatic idealism and a distinct gift for the spoken word ("my *haole* mouth," he called it), who was Judiciary spokesman at the legislature. The island-born and bred Okuda, whose special areas of responsibility were district court operations and behind-the-scenes work at the legislature, claimed no one could present legislative testimony better than Cingcade. For his part, Cingcade asserted that Okuda's long years within bureaucratic systems had not turned him into the trite civil servant: "He is exciting to watch because he is creative and refuses to be stereotyped."[12] During each legislative session, all three men kept in touch with each other, by beeper phone when necessary; it was not unusual to see the Chief Justice in the legislative corridors when summoned by his lieutenants late at night.

Okuda was no less skilled than Cingcade in getting his meaning across. He merely did so in less conventional and acceptable ways. Okuda's forte at the Legislature was the hallway encounter, where he was quick to offer information, a funny vignette, a cigarette (and he knew every legislator's favorite brand). He was especially effective with old-time, old-style politicians. Okuda's approval had some consequence for legislators: he was able to conjure up at a moment's notice hundreds of volunteer sign-holders and flag-wavers in support of a political candidate; in addition, he was an influential member of a voluntary club of district court personnel whose efforts would be useful in fund-raising.

Typical of Okuda's unorthodox approach to presentation of the Judiciary's budget request at the legislature was an annual luncheon *luau,* a feast of local foods, to which legislative finance committee members were invited. The food was bought, prepared, and served by a cross-section of Judiciary employees. Even more unusual was the entertainment at the *luau,* a summary of the Judiciary's budget request in song and dance. Okuda himself had put together the first musical show in 1970. One of his earliest presentations enumerating the Judiciary's requests was done to the tune "I Left My Heart in San Francisco"; this he did wearing a T-shirt which read "Sans Funds, Fiasco." As years passed, the performances included more singers, *hula* dancers and elaborate lyrics sung in later years to a local island tune, "The Wonderful World of Aloha."[13]

Comments about the Judiciary's clout at the Legislature began to crop up from time to time, provoking accusations of "judicial empire-building." The end of the 1970s and beginning of the 80s saw a rash of these accusations, particularly when the courts' capital improvements program began to fall into place after fifteen years of planning: on Oahu, Kauikeaouli Hale, an 11-story, 18 courtroom district court building, was completed; and Kaahumanu Hale, a 4-story, 27 courtroom circuit court building was funded and nearly completed at the end of Richardson's tenure. Plans for court buildings on the outer islands were firmed and monies allocated. Motivated by his strong sense of history and desire to preserve an historical structure, the Chief Justice began restoration work on Ali'iolani Hale, the Supreme Court building which had served also as home for the Legislative Assembly from 1874 to 1892.[14]

The accusations were exacerbated by a public call for fiscal restraint during 1982 and 1983 by the Executive Branch to all of its departments. The call for restraint was received amidst some confusion, for not all financial experts viewed the condition of State coffers with the same pessimism as the Governor's budget analysts. Competition for funds caused some tension and uneasiness among government departments and branches.[15]

As different as they were, Cingcade and Okuda had a

common reaction to innuendoes that the Judiciary was interested in "empire-building." As little as they had in common, they shared some traits requisite to an effective administrator: a belief in themselves (which sometimes could be perceived as egotism); a certain toughness (which sometimes could be interpreted as callousness); a sense of humor (which sometimes could be seen as perversity).

They also shared a stubborn unwillingness to give in to public demands and judgments that they felt were unjust. In this case, however, conversations with Richardson convinced them that a quieter profile was the order of the day at the legislature, and their presentations became a little more low-keyed.

Cingcade had not been the Chief Justice's first choice for administrative director. That honor had fallen to Bill Hiraoka, a quiet, unassuming friend from University days. The friendship between Hiraoka and Richardson blossomed when their brides found they had much in common: the shared activities of the newlywed period—picnics and card games—in time expanded to include children's birthday parties, then athletic events, then high school graduations. In 1966, Hiraoka was busy building his insurance company and he decided that it was not a good time to move into another venture, no matter how challenging it seemed and how much he wanted to work with his friend Bill Richardson.[16]

Richardson then turned to Cingcade.

Cingcade long maintained that he never would have been asked to become the courts' administrative director had it not been for Amy Ching Richardson. She was the one who had pushed for his appointment when Hiraoka decided he would not take the post. (Amy's sister Barbara was a teacher at Mid-Pacific Institute, a co-ed, secondary boarding school where Cingcade taught and was dean of students from 1961 to 1966; it was she who introduced him to Bill and Amy.)

Cingcade had worked in Richardson's 1962 lieutenant governor's campaign and, as a bachelor with no family responsibilities, he often had taken on the task of driving Amy to some political get-togethers while Bill was attending other evening functions.

Bright and quick-witted, restless, intellectually curious, Cingcade never entirely lost his school teacher's bent. He read widely. He enjoyed good talk. He sought and maintained friendships with a range of persons including university faculty, sometimes offering them short-term contracts on behalf of the Judiciary for the benefit of their expertise.

"Fat Boy" was born Toichi Okuda in the small plantation town of Kapoho, in the Puna district on the Big Island. After he moved to Honolulu, then to Chicago for a short while, to complete commercial courses at the Honolulu Business College and at Gregg School, more and more people began to call him Tom or "Fat Boy," the name Toichi being somewhat difficult to pronounce.

Slipper-shod feet, a sheriff's badge at his belt loop, a logo-ed jacket thrown over his patchwork vest (advertising "Island Termite, Inc." and "Aikane Foundation"), a cigar, a baseball cap—these were a standard part of his appearance. Okuda wore the badge because after the Sheriff's Office was attached to the District Courts in 1975, he was instrumental in expanding its functions and was proud to be a deputized sheriff.[17] It was the kind of operation that he was comfortable with, exuding as it did the machismo typically associated with any small town sheriff's office.

The machismo was also manifest in a steady stream of profanities, indiscriminately deployed with little regard for the listener's rank or station. (Okuda *was* careful with his language in front of youngsters, but they seemed to be the only ones who escaped his earthiness.)

Between them, Cingcade and Okuda provided the perfect foil for Richardson, alternately stepping forward to say things that a Chief Justice should not say and providing background support for their leader.

Privately, Bill Richardson at first had expressed some dismay with Okuda's demeanor, feeling that Okuda, who was not a typical representative of Judiciary staff, might be perceived as such by the public. Very quickly, Richardson came to realize that the behavior, like the clothing, served as a consciously-developed trademark, a means of asserting personal identity. It did not take long for him to learn that Okuda—and Cingcade—were fierce loyalists. No matter what their personal idiosyncrasies, they would never knowingly embarrass either The Boss, as they called him, or the institution he symbolized. That realization was enough to satisfy Richardson, who was unusually generous and accepting of human foibles in any case. ("Don't underestimate Tom," Richardson would say in later years. "He comes in like a yokel from Napoopoo, spewing obscenities, but under that baseball cap is a shrewd mind.[18] After a few minutes of conversation, he knows exactly who you are. And he has details about his buildings and programs and people right at his fingertips.")

Cingcade was tall, Okuda short. Cingcade's usual outward demeanor was serious, Okuda's comic. Cingcade's natural speech was literate, Okuda's "local." Their staff, their supervisory mode, and the general atmosphere of their work places reflected their different personalities. Cingcade's staff tended to be young, formally educated, eager to be in touch with national trends and at the cutting edge in court matters. Okuda's staff generally had a longer history of bureaucratic experience, a greater tendency to take a "good ole boy" approach to its work. Cingcade was a laissez-faire manager, giving initial direction and stepping in again only if problems developed. Even the occasional worker who was not sure he liked the administrative director granted that he was not a meddler. Okuda was not a meddler either, but his managerial style—like his island-based, island-bound political style—was more personalized than Cingcade's. His subordinates with any kind of ambition knew better than to grouse even in the most private of times, for his eyes and ears were everywhere.

Probably no where else but in a Richardson-led organization would persons as unalike as Cingcade and Okuda work so well, so closely, and so willingly with one another. No one would know what concessions and accommodations they made to each other in the course of their years together, but their relationship was proof of Richardson's talent for sensing a person's interests and abilities, for defying conventional job requirements when giving assignments to his employees, and for showing and, in return, eliciting high personal and professional loyalty.

Okuda, who tended to speak picturesquely and in italics, explained his loyalty to Richardson, to the Office of the Chief Justice, and to the institution of the Judiciary: "I would never, never, *never* embarrass the C.J. Look, I'm no angel, and the halo I wear around here sometimes feels so tight that I get an 'Excedrin' headache. I wish I had *more* larceny in my heart. I may act in ways that call attention to myself, but my goal is *not* self-aggrandizement. My goal is to do the *best* I know how to do for The Boss and for the Judiciary."[19]

Cingcade's loyalty was unflagging and was demonstrated in countless, conventional, day-to-day activities. At the end of their sixteen years together, Richardson was quick to name Cingcade as one of his most valuable advisors: "Les knows this court system better than anyone else, and I trust him implicitly."[20]

Not only did loyalty flow between the Chief Justice and his individual employees, but it flowed even among the most diverse of workers, one to the other, each being made to feel by Richardson that everyone was a necessary part of a family. Even as the number of Judiciary workers grew from 460 in 1966 to more than 1000 in 1982, Richardson was able to maintain a personal closeness with every employee, or at least to convey an impression to every employee (and to many attorneys as well) that the Chief Justice knew exactly who he was and what kind of job he was doing. This Richardson did in a number of ways: sending birthday greeting to court employees, playing in a baseball league with other judges, lawyers and court staff; knowing or at least seeming to know, the names and personal circumstances of everyone with whom he came in contact. If he might not have known actual names, he in fact *did* know the person, for one of his axioms was that every initial hire was important especially in a government bureaucracy; the clerk today in time rose to became a supervisor, and if he was not capable as a clerk, chances were that he would not be a capable supervisor.

Just as Bill Richardson's strong personal convictions lay at the core of some decisions rendered by the Court which he led, so did the daily tenor and achievements of his administrative leadership bear the mark of his personality.

Richardson's philosophy was simple: "I know where I want to go. I know I can't get there by myself. I'm usually able to find people who have the energy and expertise to get me there." However simple, it is a philosophy that can be effected only by a person with an ability to read people, someone with enormous charm and great powers of gentle persuasion.

Some of his law clerks over the years matter-of-factly admitted that their "CJ's" forte was not intellectualism or legal scholarship; almost to a person their feeling was, "So what of it? Our CJ never pretended or even aspired to be the greatest scholar in the legal world." When pressed for a description of Richardson's strongest trait as a leader or for an explanation of their continuing and emotional devotion to him, their responses invariably touched upon his interpersonal skills. Then, atypically for law clerks, they would resort to imprecise, uncrystallized language, as if reflecting the highly intuitive and charismatic nature of Richardson's personality and leadership.

Intuitive and charismatic leadership, by its very definition, defies rational and systematic explanation. The only gauge of its effectiveness lies in its tangible and measurable products. And any review of administrative developments during the Richardson years offers evidence that Hawaii's achievements in court management were considerable indeed.

---

1. Statement of William S. Richardson, in a personal interview, Honolulu, Hawaii, Feb. 11, 1982.

2. Statement of Lester E. Cingcade, in a conversation, Honolulu, Hawaii, June 8, 1982.

3. Statement of Tom Okuda, in a personal interview, Honolulu, Hawaii, April 7, 1983.

4. Among the incorporating directors were Louis H. Burke (California), Robert W. Calvert (Texas), James S. Holden, Chairman (Vermont), Paul C. Reardon (Massachusetts), Morell E. Sharp (Washington). Other members of the original steering committee included U.S. Supreme Court Justice Tom C. Clark, Orrison S. Marden, Earl F. Morris, and Gerald C. Snyder, members of the American Bar Association and other law-related bodies.

5. *Managing the Hawaii Judiciary: An Era of Accomplishment,* National Center for State Courts, Western Regional Office, San Francisco, California, December, 1982. Other studies completed by the Center specifically for Hawaii included *Hawaii Guidebook for Video-Taping* in 1975; two studies of Hawaii's jury system in 1976; and a review of Hawaii's annual report and statistical reporting system in 1981.

6. Statement of law clerks and various court personnel in interviews and conversations conducted in Honolulu, Hawaii, during the period of Jan., 1982 to Dec., 1983.

7. Newspaper articles of the time detail Richardson's success at reducing

trial court delay, e.g., *Honolulu Advertiser,* Oct. 14, 1966; Dec. 9, 1966; Jan. 15, 1967; Feb. 1, 1967; Feb. 3, 1967. In time, as the number of lawyers and litigation grew dramatically nationwide, heavy caseload once again became a problem in Hawaii; at the end of Richardson's tenure, caseload was a much more serious problem than it was in 1966.

8. Statements of staff members in interviews and conversations conducted in Honolulu, Hawaii, during the period of Jan., 1982 to Dec., 1983.

9. Richardson, William S. "Remarks on an Alternative Proposal to Remedy Appellate Court Congestion in Hawaii," 14 *Hawaii Bar Journal,* Summer, 1978, p. 55.

10. *Honolulu Advertiser,* Sandra Oshiro, July 21, 1978.

11. *Comprehensive Planning in the Hawaii Judiciary,* Hawaii State Judiciary, Honolulu, Hawaii, 1981.

12. Statements of Tom Okuda and Lester E. Cingcade, in separate personal interviews, Honolulu, Hawaii, April 17, 1983, and May 30, 1982, respectively.

13. Sample lyrics:

Mahalo [thank you] for all that you gave us, and thank you for listening again.

We knew that we could count on you to come through.

A need that is met is a blessing, and we know you'll try to meet ours.

You are such glorious leaders, thanks again.

We need your help once more, again. *Kokua* [help] please. *Kokua* please.

We need a judge on Oahu, to service the Circuit Court.

We need your help on all islands, all islands.

So listen please, *e ha awe mai,* [please give], all the things that we ask. All the things that we, things that we, ask of you.

(From the files of Clyde Namuo and Harriet Schimmelfennig, district court staff, who played a large role in writing and presenting the budget in song.)

14. Again, the Chief Justice appointed citizens to an "advisory committee" to guide restoration and to gain public support. Co-chaired by two women with far-reaching community influence—Evanita Midkiff and Margaret Kidwell—the committee's primary value was its ability to garner support for the restoration, particularly in business, educational, and legislative circles. Judiciary historian Jane Silverman was responsible for obtaining grants for the history center projected as part of restoration; she kept in close touch with restoration activity. Committee members included attorney Clinton Ashford, educator Gladys Brandt; businessman Kenneth F.

Brown; community volunteer Carol S. Dodd; interior designer Charles Heen; district judge Robert Klein; City and County registrar Eileen K. Lota, businesman James Morgan, Jr.; educator Laurel Kamaile Schultz; educator Elaine Takenaka; Hawaiian Government Employees Association head David K. Trask, Jr.; newspaper publisher Thurston Twigg-Smith; community worker Janet Wimberly; and museum specialist John S. Wright.

15. See, e.g., *Honolulu Advertiser,* Feb. 17, 1983 article, typical of articles between Jan. and May, 1983. Representatives of the Executive Branch toured the new district court building and they commented on what they thought were excessively large offices for judges. Upon hearing of their comments, Cingcade—normally a circumspect man in public—retorted: "Tell them wise, far-reaching decisions cannot be written in small closets."

16. Hiraoka would eventually become president of Island Insurance Co., Ltd., and National Mortgage and Finance Co., Ltd.

17. For a while, Okuda recruited several volunteer reservists including a few legislators; these reservists primarily were used to provide unpaid prisoner transport assistance between islands. Okuda viewed this use of manpower an effective and economical solution to the expensive problem of inter-island prisoner movement.

18. Napoopoo is a small village on the Big Island of Hawaii.

19. Statement of Tom Okuda, in a personal interview, Honolulu, Hawaii, April 17, 1983.

20. Others named by Richardson as trusted advisors came from an interesting variety of backgrounds: business executive and civic leader Herbert Cornuelle; close personal friend and businessman Hung Wo Ching; newspaper owner Chinn Ho; businessman William Hiraoka; long-time political and judicial associate Herman Lum; and Hai Kamakau, a trained social worker who served as Richardson's secretary and administrative assistant for many years. Statement of William S. Richardson, in a personal interview, Honolulu, Hawaii, Feb. 11, 1982.

Photo Identification

Chapter V, p. 110

The administrative "triumvirate" consisting of, from l., Lester Cingcade, Chief Justice Richardson, and Tom "Fat Boy" Okuda towards the end of 1982.

"You're not the judge of your destiny."

William S. Richardson
March 19, 1966[1]

VI
The Island Heritage

Amy Ching Richardson's death on May 1, 1975, was not totally unexpected. Yet, its effects upon her husband were no more diminished for being expected.

Beatrice Burns, the Governor's wife, referred to Amy's congenital cystic kidney condition as the "sword of Damocles," an ever-present reminder of life's precariousness. Mrs. Burns later would remark that the death of her good friend Amy seemed a double cruelty to her for it followed the Governor's death by less than a month.[2]

On March 17, 1975, just five days before a massive stroke which would hospitalize her until her death, Amy—with Bill—had paid the First Lady a call upon their return from a mainland trip, an extremely happy trip despite the prearranged visits to various hospitals for dialysis treatments. After the March 7 Honolulu wedding of daughter Corinne ("Reenie") to Stuart Wolfe (who had clerked for the Chief Justice), the Richardsons had spent some time travelling to see daughter Barbara ("Bebe") in her first year at Hastings Law School and son Billy at the University of California at Santa Barbara. Amy, after realizing the seriousness of her kidney and hypertensive situation, privately had expressed the hope that she could live to see her children well on their way in life.[3] Perhaps premonition had played a part in the Richardsons' decision to spend time with their children on the mainland.

According to Mrs. Burns, Amy was refreshed and very lively during their visit. Then, in the early hours of the next morning, Amy was taken in an ambulance to Queen's Hospital, where for more than a month, she remained conscious but unable to talk, communicating only by gestures such as nodding or shaking her head. She became unconscious for the last two weeks before her death, her vital signs at a low ebb except for a period immediately after Bebe and Billy returned from the mainland and spoke to her in her apparently unconscious state.[4]

One can imagine the effect that the "sword of Damocles" had upon Amy's internal life and interpersonal relationships —the moments of anguish and the increasingly bittersweet quality of her last years. She apparently had decided to shield her family, including her husband, from various stages of her illness as much as she could. Two years before her death, recovering in the hospital from surgery, Amy called Ruth Hiraoka, openly crying about her illness for the first and only time in their long, close friendship: "Don't tell Bill about my call. It would devastate him to know I've fallen apart over the prospect of dialysis." It seemed to Ruth that the start of dialysis for Amy symbolized the beginning of the most final stages of her life. (In a superstitious way, Amy had expected to die when she was 47—the same age that her mother was when she had died—and she regarded every additional year after 47 as a blessing. She died when whe was 54.)

The Chief Justice, known among his closest friends for his ability to deny realities which he did not wish to face, kept expressing his belief even during the last days of Amy's life that she would become well again. Ruth, who had promised

Amy that she would do so, begged him to let Amy go, for she clearly had reached a point where she was being kept alive by machines. Weeping, the Chief Justice refused to consider the request. Then, whatever private words the Chief Justice spoke to his unconscious wife, she died peacefully two days later.[4]

Bill Richardson was inconsolable at Amy's death, consumed by a grief which retained its intensity long after his wife's death. The usual descriptions of grievous loss sustained by a loving mate became understatement when applied to the Chief Justice after his wife's death.

Never a talkative man, he became less so. Often, and sometimes unexpectedly, he would lapse into silences; these silences could occur mid-conversation or even mid-sentence. Unbeknownst to most people, he visited Amy's gravesite daily for the next three years or so, usually during his lunch hour. Court personnel who travelled on business trips with him came to expect that he would go to Amy's grave immediately upon his return to Honolulu, even before he went home. A long-time friend and associate described the Richardson marriage this way: "I have never seen a more perfect alter ego than Amy was to Bill."[5] If this were the case, then a part of Bill Richardson and the core of his "home" truly did lie beneath Amy's grave marker.

So strong was Amy's presence, even in death, that not only the Chief Justice, but friends and family, even young law clerks (many of whom considered themselves "family"), referred to her in ordinary conversation, and in the most normal and natural of terms.

"Amy, who had met Bill as she was watering the lawn and he was walking home after work from the bus stop, had this advice for young girls: 'Go out and water your yard. You never know what will happen.' "[6]

"The same trait was both Bill's greatest strength and

greatest weakness: his soft, warm loving-kindness. It drew people to him. It also sometimes kept him from making the hard decisions that every leader must make. Amy helped him be tough."[7]

"Besides being smart, Amy had a confidence often found in people who come from families of accomplishment and money."[8]

Amy Ching Richardson had been born into a family that was affluent and established when measured against island norms of the day. Her father worked at Bishop Bank, ending his career at a management level usually closed to non-Caucasians. Her mother, sponsored at Punahou School and Wellesley College by the Withingtons, a wealthy family for whom she worked as a housegirl, was schooled—both socially and academically—beyond the place traditionally reserved for one of her race and family station. Amy herself spent summers at the Withington's Tantalus home with "Uncle Paul" and his family; the circumstances of her early life put her into contact with a wider, more sophisticated range of people than did Bill Richardson's. (There had been some initial resistance against the courtship on the part of the Ching family. "Amy," her sisters Barbara and Marietta would yell when the future Chief Justice called for her, "it's the boy from the other side of the tracks who used to steal our mangoes when he was a little kid.")[9]

In speaking of the different socio-economic levels of their families, Bill Richardson would say: "She was a YWCA girl; I was a locker room boy. Her family was even Republican, for heaven's sake!" Thus, one aspect of their marital relationship was a dependence of husband upon wife to provide a bridge into other worlds.

The dependency was not readily apparent, especially in their later years together, when Bill Richardson had achieved a strong public identity of his own, but it remained ever-present, causing a few close friends to suggest that in many respects, Amy really was more than alter ego: she was life force and intellectual energy to her husband.

In many marriages, the imbalances caused by the different backgrounds of the partners can chafe and irritate in time. Not so in the Richardson marriage for, according to her close fiends: "Amy simply adored Bill." Amy met the usual requirements asked of a public figure's wife; in addition, she was aide, tutor, and liaison to many worlds for her husband. But, in the inexplicable and indefinable chemistry of exchange between marital partners, her needs also were filled in an equal amount by what her husband gave to her.

Her death shocked the balance and equanimity which had become such an easy and natural part of Bill Richardson's adult life.

A touch of what some call "luck," others "providence," still others "synchronicity" seems to grace some lives more than others.

A few observers would attribute much of Bill Richardson's success to luck: the luck of being in the right place at the right time, of being of the "right" race (more than once, Richardson referred to himself as the "token Hawaiian" in the early core of Democrat leaders), and of marrying the "right" woman. Even his friends sometimes would marvel at the unlikely and unexpectedly felicitous way that people, places and events would come together in the Chief Justice's life.

Indeed, few people have so many "exceptions" made for them. Among the most notable in Richardson's life occurred at the end of his sixteen years on the bench. Then, the Chief Justice—who himself had instigated controversy in the past by announcing some Supreme Court appointments to the Bishop Estate—would be named Bishop Estate trustee amidst some controversy.

For the most part, public reaction to the idea of William Richardson as trustee was favorable; he was a logical person to serve on the five-member board which would oversee the future development of Princess Pauahi Bishop's legacy to the children of Hawaii. His name had cropped up in many quarters over the years as a potential trustee.

The controversy over his appointment centerd on two points: first, that it seemed a conflict of interest to have the appointee himself be a member of the appointing body; and secondly, that it was unusual to grant the new trustee a term of ten years (Richardson was then 63 years old) instead of until age 70, the limit that had been established by the Supreme Court in its three most recent appointments.

A November 8, 1982 news release announcing Richardson's appointment touched on the first point. When it became apparent that the Chief Justice was a viable candidate for the trusteeship, the release stated, other members of the Supreme Court asked that he remove himself from selection deliberations.[10] There was no public comment either by Richardson or the other justices about the unusual ten-year term.

When asked privately about the exception that was made for him as far as length of term was concerned, Richardson would talk about the difficulty in a large organization of getting anything of real substance done in less than ten years; one needed at least that if one were to have real impact. Inside sources later said quietly that Richardson did not ask formally for the appointment, his candidacy being a popular one and raised by many people in many circles; he *did,* however, ask for the ten-year term. One appointing justice commented privately: "How could we deny the Chief Justice an extra three years, especially when Mrs. Bishop's will itself sets no age or term limits and, until recently, appointments had been made for life?"[11]

Bill Richardson officially left the bench on December 30,

1982. His trusteeship at the Bishop Estate began on January 1, 1983. On January 21, again amidst some controversy, another exception of sorts was made for him when the University of Hawaii Board of Regents named the law school after him.

Most of the expressed public sentiment was favorable; a few disgruntled voices could be heard questioning the wisdom of going against precedent by naming a State institution after a still-living person. Part of the complaint involved the expeditiousness with which action was taken. A committee which coordinated the effort to name the school the William S. Richardson School of Law acted in an extraordinarily efficient manner to place its motion before the necessary bodies for approval.[12] The Board of Regents vote was unanimous.

One of the axioms of power is that, once attained, even those who earlier protested its abuse often give in to a natural impulse. They wield their new authority with an increasing assurance which grows into the same absoluteness they decried in others.

Along with his contemporaries in the struggle for recognition and equality in a once-elitist island community, Bill Richardson followed this pattern of behavior. As he did so, he deserved his critics' charge that he was "political." The charge was evidenced in many tendencies: to name friends to judicial boards and commissions, to appoint former law clerks to judgeships, to use his influence in ways large and small to support those with like philosophy. The realities of power and human nature *did* intrude into the supposedly dispassionate world of jurisprudence, and Richardson *did* use all the power he could to realize his goals.

For Richardson was a loyalist above all else, consistently faithful to friends and allies, to his party cause, to his personal vision, to his place of nativity. These loyalties *did* get the better of his judgment, demonstrating what is, perhaps, the first principle of friendship and—at varying levels, in varying degrees—proof of emotional commitment.

At a birthday party traditionally held for him by his past and present law clerks, surrounded by those who loved and understood him, Richardson once jokingly declared with more than a hint of truth: "I believe in nepotism."[13] Loyal himself, he understood and rewarded loyalty in others; those who worked with him toward common goals became part of his family, his *ohana.*[14]

His plans for the Law School evolved out of Richardson's loyalty to local youngsters with whom he most identified, those from families for whom lack of education was another reason for powerlessness. Richardson Court decisions which were most unacceptable to legal traditionalists were not based upon the usual, reasonably developed case precedent. Rather, these decisions stemmed from loyalty to a notion of "fairness" as the Richardson-led Court defined it.

Richardson's definition of fairness invariably reflected a deep-seated, almost atavistic, desire to correct imbalances caused by old wrongs, especially those done to the islands' indigenous peoples. Of course, what seemed "fair" to him did not seem so to persons who were used to certain expectations, for instance, businesses which had come to depend upon certain legal continuities.

The activist Chief Justice believed in the Court's authority to shape a community where all citizens would be assured of equal treatment, where both its "haves" and "have-nots" would have equal access to power and self-validation. If, in the process of building that community, some historical precedent needed reversal, if former "haves" were excluded from their usual prerogatives, then so be it.

Carried to excess through ethnic politics, this attitude can become a reverse racism of sorts, an example of non-*haole* elitism. And, in fact, a number of persons were made uncomfortable by some Richardson statements that seemed to border on excess, whether they were about native Hawaiian dispossession or "localism" as set against new immigrations to the islands. In part, the intensity of Richardson's formal statements depended upon the individual zealousness of his cadre of law clerks and speechwriters. But whatever their intensity, his speeches, written opinions and, of course, his own informal remarks, invariably reflected his basic impulse toward *ho'oponopono,* correction of old social and political wrongs.

What kept this impulse in check was Richardson's sense of balance, the almost-subconscious pull of patience, self-restraint and moderation upon other aspects of his personality. Intuition played no small part in his make-up, for mere verbal ability was not especially prized in most island neighborhoods of Richardson's day. In fact, too sure a grasp on language, glibness and talkativeness—especially in males—were suspect. *Waha,* the Hawaiian word which referred to a mouthy person, was not used as a compliment.

Unlike cultures which rely heavily upon language to shape reality, the early amalgamation of non-Western cultures in Hawaii seemed not to place great value on words and the ability to employ words with skill. The roots of this condition may have been lack of a common language base among the various ethnic groups. It may have been the Polynesian and Oriental acceptance of heightened feelings and intuition as valid means of communication.

Whatever its cause, Richardson—like many of his island peers—long retained the effects of a childhood where communication was largely visual and tactile, non-verbal and intuitive. It was not until a generation beyond Richardson's day that island youngsters would be trained into the more Western perception of language as reality, a technique of definition and revelation.

Of course, in time, with increased contact with the world

outside the neighborhoods of his youth, Richardson developed a more than adequate respect for and ability in the conventional, more Occidental uses of language. His forte and habit, however, remained that which was produced by the island milieu of his day, when language usage was marked by restraint, understatement, by silences sometimes eloquent. As a consequence, Richardson became a fairly shrewd reader of non-verbal clues which disclose character, non-language indices which mark the meaning of events.

In describing his long years in public service, friends and foes alike comment on his capacity for mediation between utterly polarized groups and individuals in order to reach a goal. A great part of that ability rested on his recognition of what motivated different persons. Sometimes slow with verbal responses, he was quick to sense what made people tick. He honed in on one person's need for social acclaim, on another's willingness to work without public kudos, on yet another's propensity for defending new ideas or for becoming a hatchet man if necessary. He sensed when infighting was unavoidable and even useful.

"For success, every movement needs all kinds of persons," he would say, placing each worker in a spot suited for his or her skills, thereby increasing the odds for success of the project at hand.

Without an instinct for bloodletting, he let others take necessary cut-throat actions. Although not as artless as he seemed, he preferred others to meet the political necessities of calculated machinations and intentional ambiguities. Not a legal scholar himself, he allowed others to find the intellectual support for his positions.

His skill was to know what needed to be done and to find the right combination of people to do it. His talent was to bridge differences between and among people so that a degree of collegiality developed out of diversity of viewpoint.[15] His ability was to simplify and translate for others his lifelong vision of community without the usual limitations of class.

Any attempt to describe a person and to measure his success ends with a degree of failure, for the skein of contradictions within every individual makes accurate definition an impossibility, and the assessment of a "successful" life depends to a degree on the values of the assessor.

Even during his single-minded pursuit of goals which remained relatively unchanged over the years, Bill Richardson displayed a panoply of traits interesting in their contradictions.

He was, and remains, an agent of change who values the past. An activist who understands the uses and meanings of tradition. A nativist who curbs ethnocentric leanings through a wide vision of the world. A flexible pragmatist who demonstrates unswerving adherence to ideals. A deceptively uncomplicated man who holds a simple, yet profound, vision of his island community. An uncommon man who somehow symbolizes a whole island generation of "common" folk, of dispossessed natives, of disenfranchised immigrants.

In the end, Bill Richardson's parents may have offered the best assessment, one which could be applied to that whole island generation of "ordinary" people who collectively—and sometimes individually—achieved extraordinary success, whatever their ethnicity. In their lifetimes, they earned a goodly measure of self-respect and of recognition from others as a viable power.

On his deathbed, just before the final heart attack which would end his life, Papa Richardson turned to his wife and said with typical island understatement, "Our *pake*-Hawaiian-*haole* kids—they didn't turn out too bad, eh?"

1. *Honolulu Star-Bulletin,* Bobbie Conlan, March 19, 1966.

2. Statement of Beatrice Burns, in a personal interview, Honolulu, Hawaii, May 28, 1982.

3. Reenie, an adoptive daughter, shared her mother's artistic interests and abilities. Bebe and Billy became lawyers, Billy graduating from the law school at Duke University. All three graduated from Punahou School, their mother's high school alma mater.

4. Statement of Ruth Hiraoka, in a personal interview, Honolulu, Hawaii, Dec. 20, 1983.

5. Statment of Lester E. Cingcade, in a personal interview, Honolulu, Hawaii, Oct. 20, 1982.

6. Statement of William Hiraoka, in a conversation, Honolulu, Hawaii, July 23, 1983.

7. Statement of a Supreme Court justice, in a conversation, Honolulu, Hawaii, Sep. 29, 1983.

8. Statement of Hai Kamakau, in a personal interview, Honolulu, Hawaii, Dec. 17, 1982.

9. Statement of William S. Richardson, in a personal interview, Honolulu, Hawaii, May 26, 1982.

10. Released from the files of the Hawaii State Judiciary's Public Information Office. See also *Honolulu Star-Bulletin,* Nov. 8, 1982.

11. Statement of a Supreme Court justice, in a conversation, Honolulu, Hawaii, Dec. 22, 1983.

12. Committee members included attorney Donn Carlsmith, chairman; court administrator Lester Cingcade; court deputy director Tom Okuda; the Chief Justice's son William K. Richardson; former assistant to John A. Burns, Mary Isa; and attorneys Nathan Aipa, Ivan Lui-Kwan, Stanford Manuia, and Bambi Weil.

13. Statement of Richardson law clerks, in a conversation, Dec. 1982.

14. The Hawaiian *ohana* refers to the concept of family, based either on blood or feeling of kinship.

15. He was able to do this even in High Courts marked by the occasional prickly personality. In one Court, when tensions ran so high that communication took place largely by memo between two of its members, Richardson was able to hold the justices together.

Photo Identification
Chapter VI, p. 128
A photo of Chief Justice Richardson taken in his chambers at the end of his tenure in late 1982 and a photo of his wife taken by the Chief Justice himself in the early 1970s.

A Note About Sources

A primary source for this work was, of course, William S. Richardson, with whom the writer held a number of informal conversations and structured interviews from 1980 to 1984. Information of a general nature gleaned during these meetings is included in the text without footnotes; more specific statements which express a point of view are pinpointed in time.

Statements of a sensitive nature made by interviewees either are not footnoted or are footnoted generically. In addition, persons who asked to be unidentified sources are not listed by name. While such practice is not regarded as high scholarship, still, this work holds no scholarly pretensions. Instead, it seeks to reach a general readership with the story of one person's life which—while uniquely personal and individual—is yet typical of the lives of many people within a certain island generation.

Sources

Published Sources: Government Documents and Publications

Address by Governor John A. Burns, Joint Session, Fourth State Legislature, General Session of 1967, Legislative Reference Bureau.

Comprehensive Planning in the Hawaii Judiciary. Honolulu: Hawaii State Judiciary, 1981.

Journal of the House of Representatives of the Fifth Legislature, State of Hawaii, Regular Session of 1969. Honolulu: [n.n.], [n.d.].

Journal of the House of Representatives of the Fifth Legislature, State of Hawaii, Regular Session of 1970. Honolulu: [n.n.]. [n.d.].

Journal of the House of Representatives of the Sixth Legislature, State of Hawaii, Regular Session of 1971. Honolulu: [n.n.], [n.d.].

Journal of the Senate of the Fifth Legislature, State of Hawaii, Regular Session of 1969. Honolulu: [n.n.], [n.d.].

Meller, Norman. "Hawaii Law School Study." Legislative Reference Bureau Report No. 3. Honolulu: University of Hawaii, 1971.

Proceedings of the Constitutional Convention of 1968. 2 vols. Honolulu: Administrator of Convention, State of Hawaii, 1972–1973.

Published Sources: Books and Pamphlets

Adler, Jacob, ed. *The Journal of Prince Alexander Liholiho: The Voyages Made to the United States, England and France in 1849–1850.* Hawaii: The University Press for the Hawaiian Historical Society, 1967.

Bird, Isabella L. *Six Months in the Sandwich Islands.* Honolulu: University of Hawaii Press for Friends of the Library of Hawaii, 1964.

Cleveland, Harlan, and Heyman, I. Michael. "Programs in Legal Education at the University of Hawaii." Honolulu: University of Hawaii, 1972.

Crawford, David Livingston. *Paradox in Hawaii: An Examination of Industry and Education and the Paradox They Present.* Boston: Stratford Company, 1933.

Erlich, Thomas, and Manning, Thomas. "Programs in Law at the University of Hawaii: A Report to the President of the University." Honolulu: [n.n.], 1970.

Holmes, Oliver Wendell. *The Common Law I (1881).* Boston: Little, Brown and Company, 1923.

Littler, Robert C. M. *The Governance of Hawaii.* California: Stanford University Press, 1929.

Managing the Hawaii Judiciary: An Era of Accomplishment. San Francisco: National Center for State Courts, Western Regional Office, 1982.

Tuttle, Daniel W., Jr. *Hawaii Voting Behavior: A Background Guide to Some Significant Characteristics of Honolulu's (Oahu's) 138 Precincts.* Honolulu: University of Hawaii Department of Political Science, 1965.

———. *Hawaii Voting Behavior: A Background Guide to Some Significant Characteristics of Honolulu's (Oahu's) 141 Precincts.* Honolulu: [n.n.], 1968.

Warren, William C., and Mearns, Edward A., Jr. "The School of Law, University of Hawaii: Its Feasibility and Social Importance." Honolulu: [n.n.], 1969.

Wills and Deeds of Trust: Bernice P. Bishop Museum, Charles R. Bishop Trust. Honolulu, Hawaii: Printshop of Hawaii Co., Ltd. 3d Ed. 1957.

Published Sources: Journals and Periodicals

Cades, J. Russell. "Judicial Legislation in the Supreme Court of Hawaii: A Brief Introduction of the 'Knowne Uncertaintie' of the Law," 7 *Hawaii Bar Journal* 58 (1978).

Published Sources: Newspapers

Honolulu Advertiser, Jan. 2, 1966; Feb. 26, 1966; March 26, 1966; Oct. 14, 1966; Nov. 15, 1966; Dec. 9, 1966; Jan. 15, 1967; Feb. 1, 1967; Feb. 3, 1967; June 7, 1968; July 31, 1968; Feb. 13, 1970; Sept. 5, 1970; June 23, 1971; June 25, 1971; June 28, 1971; June 30, 1971; Feb. 12, 1972; Feb. 14, 1974; Aug. 16, 1975; Sept. 3, 1975; Nov. 14, 1975; Nov. 28, 1975; Aug. 25, 1978; Nov. 27, 1978; Dec. 19, 1979; Feb. 17, 1980; Feb. 20, 1981; May 14, 1982; Feb. 17, 1983.

"Honolulu News," Jan. 29, 1971.

Honolulu Star-Bulletin, May 14, 1956; Sept. 3, 1960; Jan. 8, 1963; Feb. 25, 1966; March 15, 1966; March 16, 1966; March 19, 1966; March 26, 1966; Nov. 15, 1966; May 5, 1967; Feb. 29, 1968; Aug. 1, 1968; June 22, 1971; June 23, 1971; July 6, 1971; July 17, 1971; April 4, 1973; Feb. 14, 1974; Feb. 5, 1975; July 11, 1978; Dec. 26, 1978; Feb. 12, 1980; April 29, 1981; Oct. 4, 1982, Nov. 8, 1982.

Unpublished Sources: Archives of Hawaii

Correspondence from Vaughn MacCaughey, school superintendent, to Governor Charles J. McCarthy, July 1, 1920, McCarthy Papers.

Governor's Advisory Committee on Education, Survey of Schools and Industry. Honolulu: J. K. Butler, 1930–1931.

Petition from Kailua natives to Kamehameha III and the Legislature, FO & Ex., 1845.

Privy Council Minutes. July 14, 1848, Vol. 4. Aug. 15, 1948, Vol. 4.

Unpublished Sources: Miscellaneous

Hawaii State Judiciary. Files in Public Information Office.

John A. Burns Oral History Project, 1975–1976. Honolulu: [n.n.], 1975.

Richardson, William S. Speech and correspondence files.

Unpublished Sources: Personal Interviews

Burns, Beatrice. Honolulu, May 28, 1982.
Burns, James S. Honolulu, April 25, 1982 and May 26, 1982.
Cingcade, Lester E. Honolulu, June 8, 1982 and Oct. 20, 1982.
Hiraoka, Ruth. Honolulu, Dec. 20, 1983.
Hiraoka, William. Personal conversation. Honolulu, July 23, 1983.
Kamakau, Hai. Honolulu, Dec. 17, 1982.
Loomis, Lois. Telephone conversation. Honolulu, March 3, 1983.
Lum, Herman T. F. Personal conversation. Honolulu, Feb. 11, 1982.
Marumoto, Masaji. Honolulu, May 21, 1982 and May 28, 1982.
Okuda, Tom. Honolulu, April 7, 1983.
Richardson, Amy Wung. Honolulu, Sept. 2, 1971 and May 24, 1978. (Interview and conversation conducted for the Chinese History Center respectively by Dorothy Soong and Sybil Ho, then by Jane Silverman.)
Richardson, Arlon. Honolulu, Dec. 18, 1982. (Interview conducted by Scott Shirai.)
Richardson, William S. Numerous formal interviews and informal conversations. Honolulu, 1980–1984.
Wong, Grace Richardson. Honolulu, Dec. 20, 1982. (Interview conducted by Scott Shirai.)
Interviews and conversations with various judges, court staff, and law clerks to William S. Richardson, State of Hawaii, 1980–1983.

Acknowledgments

The writer wishes to acknowledge with appreciation the assistance of the following persons: Matthew S. Goodbody; Jean Imamoto at the Legislative Reference Bureau; Bea Kaya and her staff at the Hawaii Newspaper Agency Library; Brian Nakamura; Jane L. Silverman; John E. Simonds; Kimi Sugamura; and Norris Tanigawa.

Index